N CAMP

PASSPORT

A framework for personal and social development

Commissioned by the Calouste Gulbenkian Foundation

Jane Lees and Sue Plant

 CALOUSTE GULBENKIAN FOUNDATION, LONDON

Authors' acknowledgements

We would like to thank Simon Richey, Director of the Gulbenkian Foundation's Education Programme, for his astute foresight in recognising the need for a coherent framework for PSE, for commissioning the project and for his tremendous support throughout. We also wish to thank John Ford of the Department for Education and Employment for his support and belief in us, as well as the Department itself for its financial assistance. We are extremely grateful to Felicity Luard of the Gulbenkian Foundation's Literary and Information Department for her considerable help during the final stages of drafting the publication and to Elizabeth Hartley-Brewer for editing the text. Last but not least, we wish to say a special thank you to Professor John Tomlinson for his wisdom, experience and supportive guidance as he chaired the Advisory Committee throughout the project.

The project has benefited enormously from the commitment of the members of the PASSPORT Advisory Committee and Reference Group, and from the involvement of all the teachers with whom we have worked in the development schools. The enthusiastic response which the fourth draft of PASSPORT received from the pilot local authorities and their schools enabled us to put forward the framework as a contribution to the revision of the national curriculum with confidence. We would like to thank them all for the role they played. We have also been extremely encouraged by all the help and support we have received from many individuals and organisations. The membership of these groups is given on pages 60–2.

Jane Lees and Sue Plant
Project leaders

The authors

Jane Lees and Sue Plant have many years experience between them in personal and social development in schools. They have been involved in teaching, curriculum development, advising, writing, inspecting and training, and have worked with teachers from schools across all phases. They are national leaders in this field: they have both served as Chair of NSCoPSE, the national PSE association. Jane is Vice-chair of the National Advisory Group for PSHE and Sue is Chair of the Sex Education Forum. They now work as independent consultants.

Extracts from this document may be reproduced for non-commercial educational purposes.

Published by the
Calouste Gulbenkian Foundation
United Kingdom Branch
98 Portland Place
London W1N 4ET
Tel: 020 7636 5313

© 2000 Calouste Gulbenkian Foundation
Reprinted 2000, 2001

The right of Jane Lees and Sue Plant to be identified as the authors of this work has been asserted in accordance with the Copyright, Designs and Patents Act 1988.

ISBN 0 903319 95 0

British Library Cataloguing-in-Publication Data
A catalogue record for this book is available from the British Library

Designed by Andrew Shoolbred
Printed by Expression Printers Ltd, IP23 8HH

Distributed by Turnaround Publisher Services Ltd, Unit 3, Olympia Trading Estate, Coburg Road, Wood Green, London N22 6TZ.
Tel: 020 8829 3000, Fax: 020 8881 5088, E-mail: orders@turnaround-uk.com

Contents

Foreword

by Professor John Tomlinson CBE
Chairman of the Advisory Committee, Professor Emeritus, University of Warwick

Working with the Advisory Committee and alongside Simon Richey, Jane Lees and Sue Plant has been an exciting and constructive experience. I believe that what we have created will be of great value to many future generations of teachers as they build the web of relationships with children which allows pupils to grow in confidence as persons and as learners.

We owe the origin to Simon Richey's insight and determination. He it was who saw, from the evidence of the many school projects the Gulbenkian Foundation had sponsored under his guidance, the vital need to help policy-makers understand better the importance of Personal and Social Education (PSE), and to give teachers ideas and processes which would bolster their confidence in its essential value and provide ways of making it happen.

Hence the Advisory Committee was born, and the wisdom of Jane Lees and Sue Plant was brought to inform its work.

We realised, in 1998, that we were at a crucial moment, because Government had decided to undertake a revision of the national curriculum. We dedicated ourselves to helping and informing that process, determined that PSE should be an integral part of the new curriculum, not an 'optional extra'. We started by identifying the best of what was already provided and producing an up-to-date document making the case for PSE (none was available). We took our early drafts to schools and LEAs in many different settings and took their advice on how it could be refined and improved. The resulting Framework Document, which we called PASSPORT, was then used in a variety of ways:

- by the National Advisory Group on Personal, Social and Health Education in preparing its Report to the Secretaries of State: *Preparing Young People for Adult Life*

- in submissions to the QCA and DfEE for their work on the national curriculum

- in shaping the supporting Guidance from Government to schools on the implementation of PSHE and citizenship in the curriculum.

Meanwhile, as a result of our consultations and the reputation PASSPORT acquired, many schools have obtained it and used it to 'spring-clean' their curriculum and processes for promoting personal and social development – teaching better, not teaching more. We also know that it has been pressed into use for both initial teacher training and in-service training. More than 1,000 copies of the fourth draft of August 1998 are already in circulation.

The Gulbenkian Foundation has now generously decided to publish PASSPORT and provide copies for every primary, secondary and special school in England, both maintained and independent. We are sure it will be widely welcomed and used, because schools are continually asking for it. It will be a valuable complement to the QCA Guidance – it is more detailed and includes case studies from schools which will be immediately recognisable and helpful to colleagues in similar situations. And LEAs and Universities and Colleges with responsibility for teacher education and training will continue to value its insights.

I end with a personal statement. A lifetime in the education service and the service of education has taught me that unless children – whatever their chronological age – are continually being helped to 'grow up', that is, to make better sense of themselves and their relationships with others, they cannot make best use of the education offered them by their teachers. Above all the human child seeks to find reassurance and meaning in life – just as do adults. It is part of the joyful task of the teacher to help them.

PASSPORT and the PSHE and citizenship frameworks

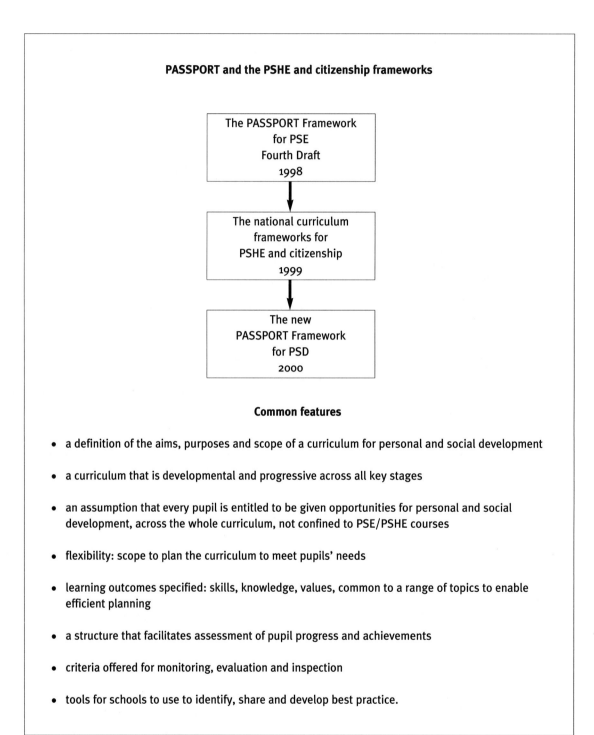

The PASSPORT Framework
for PSE
Fourth Draft
1998

↓

The national curriculum
frameworks for
PSHE and citizenship
1999

↓

The new
PASSPORT Framework
for PSD
2000

Common features

- a definition of the aims, purposes and scope of a curriculum for personal and social development

- a curriculum that is developmental and progressive across all key stages

- an assumption that every pupil is entitled to be given opportunities for personal and social development, across the whole curriculum, not confined to PSE/PSHE courses

- flexibility: scope to plan the curriculum to meet pupils' needs

- learning outcomes specified: skills, knowledge, values, common to a range of topics to enable efficient planning

- a structure that facilitates assessment of pupil progress and achievements

- criteria offered for monitoring, evaluation and inspection

- tools for schools to use to identify, share and develop best practice.

Introduction
PASSPORT: A framework for personal and social development

What is PASSPORT's origin?

The PASSPORT Framework for Personal and Social Education (PSE) was the outcome of the PASSPORT project, commissioned in 1997 by the Calouste Gulbenkian Foundation, with support from the Department for Education and Employment (DfEE). Its purpose was to raise the profile, status and quality of PSE in schools. It drew extensively on good practice in schools, and guidance from local authorities and other sources, and was published in draft form and extensively piloted in 1998. It has made a major contribution to the development of the national curriculum frameworks for PSHE and citizenship and the guidance which supports them.

Following publication of the national curriculum frameworks, the PASSPORT Framework has been revised to reflect the structure of the new frameworks and renamed 'PASSPORT: A framework for personal and social development (PSD)'.

What is in the new PASSPORT?

The new PASSPORT Framework includes:
- all strands of the national curriculum PSHE and citizenship framework at key stages 1 and 2;
- all strands of the national curriculum PSHE framework at key stages 3 and 4;
- those elements covered by the statutory order for citizenship at key stages 3 and 4 which contribute to personal and social development.

What does PASSPORT do?

The new PASSPORT Framework:
- amplifies the frameworks for PSHE and citizenship;
- complements the initial guidance for schools from QCA on PSHE and citizenship;
- provides a single framework which acknowledges curricular guidance concerned with various aspects of personal and social development.

It builds on its original intention to:
- offer teachers a comprehensive and systematic framework for implementing a curriculum for personal and social development which is easy to use, and which will enable teachers to integrate a wide range of initiatives within a coherent programme;
- draw together the common elements of the national initiatives that promote education concerning different aspects of pupils' personal and social development: health, citizenship, sex and relationships, drugs, parenthood, financial capability, safety, sustainability, work and careers;
- identify the common core of skills, knowledge and understanding, and attitudes and values which constitute the pupils' basic entitlement to personal and social development.

It will also help schools to attain the new National Healthy School Standard (NHSS), which is designed to provide a healthier working and learning environment for staff and pupils and, like PASSPORT, requires that the curriculum's underpinning principles are put into practice throughout the school.

Who is PASSPORT for?

The PASSPORT Framework for PSD is intended for:
- curriculum managers, PSHE and citizenship co-ordinators, Healthy School co-ordinators and any teacher in a primary, secondary and special school who has responsibility for co-ordinating a whole school approach to personal and social development, including PSE courses;
- local education authority advisers who provide advice and support on PSHE and citizenship to schools.

What will schools gain from using PASSPORT?

The PASSPORT Framework for PSD will help schools to:
- reflect on and organise the work they already do;
- identify good practice across the curriculum and;
- create a coherent programme of PSHE and citizenship.

1 The relationship of PASSPORT to national initiatives

This section demonstrates PASSPORT's links with national initiatives:
1 National Curriculum 2000
2 DfEE, QCA and other curriculum guidance
3 National Healthy School Standard

1 PASSPORT and National Curriculum 2000

i) How PASSPORT relates to the aims of the school curriculum

The new *National Curriculum Handbooks** set out a rationale for the school curriculum, and highlight two broad aims, reproduced below. The national curriculum provides a basis on which schools are expected to develop their own curriculum to meet these aims.

Aims for the school curriculum

- The school curriculum should aim to provide opportunities for all pupils to learn and to achieve.

- The school curriculum should aim to promote pupils' spiritual, moral, social and cultural development and prepare all pupils for the opportunities, responsibilities and experiences of life.

These two aims reinforce each other. The personal development of pupils, spiritually, morally, socially and culturally, plays a significant part in their ability to learn and achieve. Development in both areas is essential to raising standards of attainment of all pupils.

In other words, children's personal and social development is at the heart of the school curriculum, and the interdependency of the two aims is stressed:

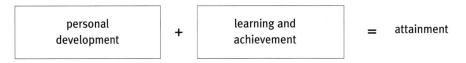

The PASSPORT Framework sets out what pupils need to learn and the opportunities education should offer to help pupils reach their full potential. A curriculum which promotes personal and social development can:

- raise pupils' confidence and self-esteem by reminding pupils and teachers of the importance of respecting everyone as an individual and appreciating effort;
- offer an especially supportive climate for learning;
- provide a foundation for acquiring the skills needed to learn and grow up at ease with oneself;
- increase pupils' motivation and deepen their understanding through providing relevant opportunities for 'real-life' learning;
- improve pupils' ability to reflect on and become responsible for their own learning;
- reduce the chances that pupils' education will be interrupted or impaired, for example, by unintended pregnancy, excessive drug misuse or fear of bullying.

* The National Curriculum: Handbook for primary teachers in England – Key stages 1 and 2, and The National Curriculum: Handbook for secondary teachers in England – Key stages 3 and 4. DfEE/QCA 1999.

ii) How PASSPORT relates to the PSHE and citizenship frameworks

There are three new national curriculum frameworks:
- PSHE and citizenship for key stages 1 and 2;
- PSHE for key stages 3 and 4;
- the statutory order for citizenship for key stages 3 and 4.

They include some elements which must be taught and others where schools can determine the content according to their needs:
- schools can decide what to teach in PSHE (and citizenship at key stages 1 and 2);
- the subject order for citizenship at key stages 3 and 4 has a statutory programme of study;
- sex and relationships education, and careers education and guidance are statutory at key stages 3 and 4, but the content is largely left to schools.

There is a clear expectation that schools will use these frameworks (set out in the two National Curriculum Handbooks already mentioned) to meet the two aims set out in i) above. Even though citizenship in secondary schools does not become mandatory until September 2002, planning for personal and social development will be coherent at key stages 3 and 4 only if PSHE and citizenship are considered in parallel.

Together, the three frameworks contain four interrelated strands which promote continuity and progression across all key stages, as shown in Fig. 1.

The PASSPORT Framework and its planning process provides schools with a coherent approach to implementing PSHE and citizenship. It covers all four strands and all three frameworks, with the exception of those statutory elements of citizenship at key stages 3 and 4 which do not contribute specifically to personal and social development.

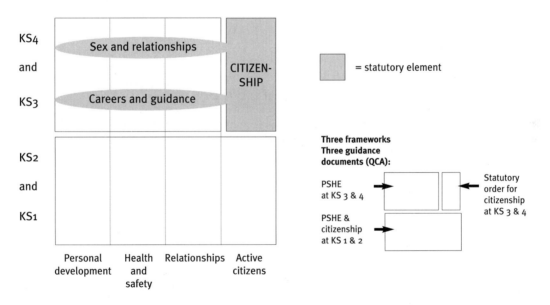

Fig. 1   *PSHE and citizenship. Three frameworks: one picture*

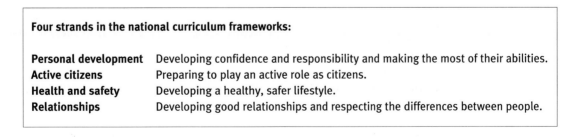

Four strands in the national curriculum frameworks:

Personal development	Developing confidence and responsibility and making the most of their abilities.
Active citizens	Preparing to play an active role as citizens.
Health and safety	Developing a healthy, safer lifestyle.
Relationships	Developing good relationships and respecting the differences between people.

2 PASSPORT and QCA, DfEE and other curriculum guidance

The PASSPORT Framework for PSD covers not only those elements of the PSHE and citizenship frameworks as described on the previous page but also relevant aspects of sex and relationships, drugs, health, financial capability, parenthood, sustainability, work and careers education that have been set out in other guidance documents.

The way in which PASSPORT relates to all these guidance documents is shown in Fig. 2.

Key points:
- The PASSPORT Framework represents a basic entitlement for pupils to a curriculum for personal and social development.
- Schools which implement the PASSPORT Framework (plus the statutory elements at key stages 3 and 4) will be meeting the requirements of the national curriculum frameworks.
- The separate guidance documents give more detailed advice about each of the specialist aspects of PSHE and citizenship. *Schools can use these to tailor their curriculum to meet the particular needs of their pupils, school and community.*

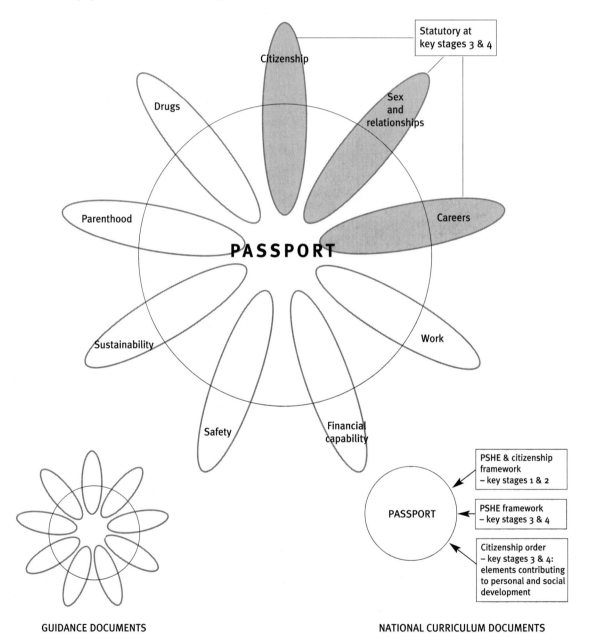

Fig. 2 The relationship between PASSPORT, the national curriculum documents and other guidance documents

PSHE and citizenship guidance documents: a checklist

PSHE

Personal, Social and Health Education and Citizenship at Key Stages 1 and 2: Initial guidance for schools. QCA 2000.

Personal, Social and Health Education at Key Stages 3 and 4: Initial guidance for schools. QCA 2000.

Preparing Young People for Adult Life. DfEE 1999.

Citizenship

Citizenship at Key Stages 3 and 4: Initial guidance for schools. QCA 2000.

Education for Citizenship and the Teaching of Democracy in Schools: Consultation paper. QCA 1998.

Sex and relationships *Sex and Relationship Education Guidance.* DfEE (draft).

Drugs

Good Practice in Drug Education and Prevention series. SCODA 1998–9.
The Right Choice: Guidance on selecting drug education materials.
The Right Approach: Quality standards in drug education.
The Right Responses: Managing and making policy for drug-related incidents in schools.

Sustainability

Education for Sustainable Development in the Schools Sector, CEE 1998.

Work

Industry and the Curriculum 5–14: Guidance for teachers. CEI 1993.

Preparation for Working Life: Guidance for schools on managing a co-ordinated approach to work-related learning at key stage 4. QCA 1999.

Careers

Learning Outcomes from Careers Education and Guidance (key stages 3 and 4, and post-16). QCA 1999.

Opening Doors: A framework for developing career-related learning in primary and middle schools. CRAC/NICEC 1999.

Skills for Choice: Developing pupils' career management skills. SCAA (QCA) 1996.

Safety

Safety Education. DfEE (forthcoming).

Financial capability

Education for Financial Capability. DfEE (forthcoming).

Parenthood

Education for Parenthood. DfEE (forthcoming).

For full references – see pages 60–1.

Schools can expect further guidance on these and other aspects of PSHE and citizenship in the future.

3 PASSPORT and the National Healthy School Standard

The PASSPORT Framework for PSD addresses curriculum planning for personal and social development. However, to implement the framework effectively, a school will also need to consider the influence of other aspects of school life on the pupils.

The new *National Healthy School Standard* (NHSS)* aims to promote mental and physical health by adopting a **whole school approach** that achieves a better match between a school's stated values and its provision. A healthy school:

- understands the importance of investing in health to assist in the process of raising the level of pupil achievement and improving standards;
- recognises the need to provide a physical and social environment that is conducive to learning;
- has the relevant structures and policies in place to support the curriculum.

i) A whole school approach to personal and social development

The NHSS programme supports PASSPORT by helping schools to consider a whole school approach shown in Fig. 3.

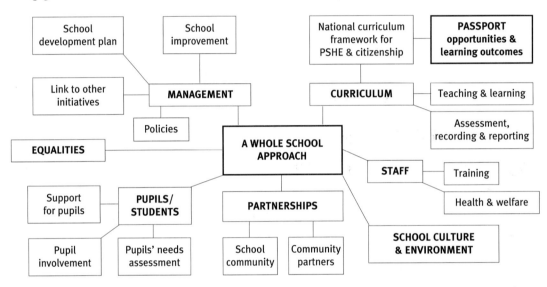

Fig. 3   A whole school approach to personal and social development

Responsibility for a whole school approach to personal and social development should be held by a senior member of staff. Schools will need to review:

- school organisation and management: for example, the extent to which pupils have opportunities to participate in decisions about their schooling, pupil representation on committees and the style of leadership in the school;

- the school environment: the condition of pupils' surroundings, the use made of playgrounds and other spaces, the quality of eating areas and the safety of the premises;

- relationships with parents and other members of the community: their involvement in the life of the school and how they may benefit from it;

- the use of people and organisations in the community: health professionals, local employers and specialist organisations among others can help pupils and extend their horizons;

- policies central to the pupils' health and wellbeing: such as PSE/PSHE, sex education, drugs, child protection, behaviour and anti-bullying, health and safety, teaching and learning, equal opportunities etc.;

A school should aim to create a safe, supportive and caring community for everyone, including pupils, staff, parents and governors.

*National Healthy School Standard: Getting Started – A guide for schools and Guidance. DfEE 1999.

ii) A whole curriculum approach to personal and social development

Planned opportunities for promoting pupils' personal and social development exist across the curriculum, not only in time designated as PSE, PSHE or circle time. Fig. 4 presents a whole curriculum model for PSD. PASSPORT identifies a range of key curricular opportunities and experiences for PSD which schools can consider as an entitlement for pupils during their school career (pages 19–21).

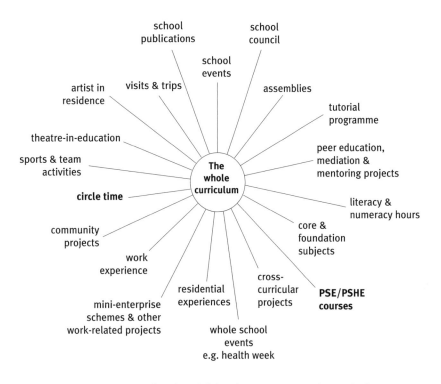

Fig. 4 Promoting personal and social development across the curriculum

Key issues for implementing a whole curriculum approach

Equality and inclusion
When considering opportunities for personal and social development across the curriculum, schools should consider whether the opportunity is open to all pupils. If an activity is for a particular class only, is voluntary, or excludes some pupils because of their special needs, it cannot properly be considered as part of the basic entitlement curriculum for PSD.

The importance of planning and reflection
Schools offer many of the opportunities in Fig. 4. However, only if these are consciously planned to exploit the potential for pupils' personal and social learning will they contribute to personal and social development. To be included in a whole curriculum approach to PSD, a curriculum activity must:
- identify the intended learning outcomes in terms of the skills, knowledge and values explored;
- provide opportunities for pupils to reflect on what they have done, how they feel, what they have learnt and what they will do next.

When pupils are asked to reflect on something they have learnt or done, whether it be subsequent to a practical activity, an outing or a lesson, they develop a crucial life skill and therefore grow in self-knowledge.

The whole school and whole curriculum approaches are the cornerstones of the Initial Guidance from QCA* to help schools to implement the new frameworks for PSHE and citizenship. This guidance points out that 'PSHE can not be confined to specific timetabled time' and that 'schools will wish to consider a variety of ways of providing citizenship in their curriculum'.

*Personal, Social and Health Education and Citizenship at Key Stages 1 and 2: Initial guidance for schools;
Personal, Social and Health Education at Key Stages 3 and 4: Initial guidance for schools and Citizenship at Key Stages 3 and 4: Initial guidance for schools. QCA 2000.

2 Planning a curriculum for PSD using the PASSPORT Framework

Step by step to a curriculum for PSD

The national curriculum frameworks for PSHE and citizenship and the PASSPORT Framework for PSD identify what pupils should be taught and should learn **at each key stage**. To use the frameworks successfully, planning must start with the needs of **pupils in each year group**.

PASSPORT has developed and piloted successfully a step-by-step implementation process.

For each year group

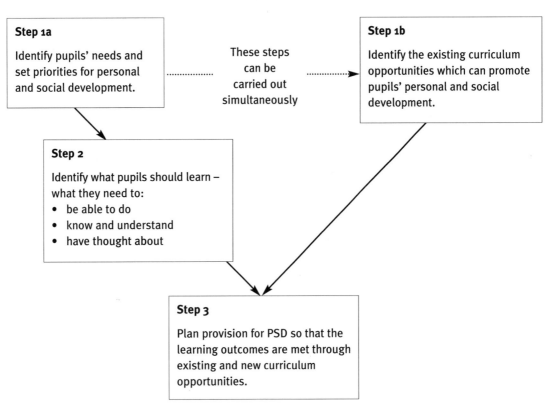

Step 1a

Identify pupils' needs and set priorities for personal and social development.

.... These steps can be carried out simultaneously ....➤

Step 1b

Identify the existing curriculum opportunities which can promote pupils' personal and social development.

Step 2

Identify what pupils should learn – what they need to:
- be able to do
- know and understand
- have thought about

Step 3

Plan provision for PSD so that the learning outcomes are met through existing and new curriculum opportunities.

- The lead responsibility for planning a curriculum for PSD should lie with a senior staff member who holds a curriculum responsibility. This will help to achieve full co-operation and flexible working throughout the school. Year or key stage co-ordinators and year heads will have an important development and monitoring role.

- The step-by-step process will take time to complete for all years, and it should feature in the school development plan. Once completed, it will only require review and adaptation.

- The curriculum for PSD should be consistent with a school's published aims. Schools may wish to review their public statements to ensure they do not conflict with or undermine curriculum aims. (see page 8).

The remainder of this section addresses the detailed application of each step. Each step involves the completion of blank forms. As these are completed, they will build into a curriculum plan for PSD for the year group in question.

Step 1a: Identify pupils' needs and set priorities for personal and social development

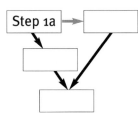

The PASSPORT Framework for PSD is not a curriculum; schools can use it to develop their own curriculum taking account of the needs of their pupils.

In developing a programme for pupils' personal and social development, schools will need to establish their own priorities. This is most effectively carried out through a **needs analysis**, as part of the review process which leads to planning.

This first step is the key to successful implementation and should not be missed out.

Conducting a needs analysis for each year group

Questions:
- At what stage of development are pupils?
- What are the milestones for this year group and the events that take place during this year?
- How much do pupils already know and what skills do they have or need?
- What can we learn from their behaviour in class and in the playground?

So what are the priorities for the pupils' learning during this year, in relation to each of the four strands within the PSHE and citizenship frameworks?

These questions can be answered by:
- consulting relevant groups of people
- using data about the school population
- consulting relevant documents

The consultation process

Setting priorities for the year group is best carried out by the year or key stage co-ordinator, or head of year, in consultation with all the relevant groups and using the latest information on pupils of that age.

The **table of pupils' needs and priorities** on page 18 can help the consultation process. It is based on a broad view of children and young people, their stages of development, and significant milestones in their lives drawn from national data.

Consulting with pupils
The following methods are effective:
- Surveys, using questionnaires and interviews, focusing on what they already know and asking what they would like to learn about, preferably to be carried out by pupils.

- Question boxes or Lucky Dip exercises enabling pupils to identify their questions and concerns anonymously.

- Draw and Write* activities: an effective way to find out what pupils know about a particular issue.

- Data from the pupils' evaluation of a project or unit of work.

- A school council may provide a forum in which to raise these issues with pupils.

The Schools Health Education Unit in Exeter will administer the standardised Health-Related Behaviour Questionnaire to a sample of pupils. The results of all the school surveys are published annually.

*Draw and Write is a technique developed by the Health Education Authority's Primary Schools Project, based at Southampton University, to research the knowledge and attitudes of primary age children throughout the UK. Details of the approach, which can be adapted for older pupils, are in Health for Life, HEA 1989.

Consulting with staff

- Discussion should start with the staff who know the pupils best, e.g. the class teachers or tutors, using the pupils' needs and priorities sheet on page 18.

- The discussion can be extended to other groups of staff who teach the year group, both subject teachers and support staff, not forgetting lunchtime supervisors.

- The Special Needs Co-ordinator holds a great deal of relevant information about the local community and the needs of its children.

Consulting with others

- Parents can help to clarify issues that pupils need to learn about. A simple tick-box questionnaire, with blanks for their own ideas, may be completed by parents while they wait for their interviews at a year group parents' meeting.

- The school nurse holds the school's health profile, which identifies annual priorities for intervention. S/he will also be familiar with the local Health Improvement Programme's health priorities for young people. If drop-in sessions are run, the kinds of issues pupils raise will provide further insight into their needs, without breaching confidentiality.

- Where schools have a Police Liaison Officer, s/he will be able to provide information about the youth crime and personal safety profile of the community.

This table lists people, agencies and documents which will help to identify pupils' personal and social needs.

	ESSENTIAL	DESIRABLE	NEED TO WATCH
Priorities	School including:	Local including:	National including:
Consult	pupils parents teachers other adults such as the school nurse	Health promotion Primary care group Sexual health services Police and safety services Careers service Education business partnership Environmental agencies	
Data and documents	Health-Related Behaviour Questionnaire: school data School health profile School Development Plan Ofsted Report	Education Development Plan Health Improvement Plan Drug Action Team priorities Youth crime profile Teenage pregnancy rate Accident rates and types Health-Related Behaviour Questionnaire: local profile	Drug Prevention Strategy Teenage Pregnancy Action Plan Sexual Health Strategy Safe Routes to School Key Skills Health Development Agency reports

The National Healthy School Standard requires schools to set their priorities for becoming a more healthy school, including implementing PSD, through a full consultation with the groups identified above and using the sources of data available to the school.

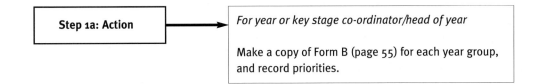

Step 1a: Action → *For year or key stage co-ordinator/head of year*

Make a copy of Form B (page 55) for each year group, and record priorities.

Pupils' NEEDS and PRIORITIES to be taken into account in developing a programme for personal and social development

	Key Stage 1	Key Stage 2	Key Stage 3	Key Stage 4
Development – physical	Need to let off steam with physical activity e.g. walking, running, swimming. Have a range of physical skills e.g. cycling, ball-handling. Have a heightened awareness of difference between the sexes.	Pubertal changes begin. Girls stronger and bigger than boys. Have good appetites – need less fat and sugar. Dental, body and foot hygiene important.	Wide range of body shape, size etc. Hormonal effects on mood. Personal hygiene more important. Body needs exercise, rest, healthy diet, regular hygiene.	Neither child nor adult. Much concern about body image especially in girls – anorexia and bulimia more prevalent. Skin complaints – acne is common. Physical activity less regular for girls.
– social	Understand rules for play, work and life, but cannot always stick to them. May not yet have team spirit. Have one or more friends but need help with social skills. Vulnerable to media messages.	Becoming sensible and sensitive to others. Know rules of the games but not always good losers. Sense of fairness developing. Being part of a group is important, normally led by a key individual. Groups tend to be unisex. Vulnerable to trends and fashion. Often lack independence. Acute awareness of fairness and injustice.	Pre-adolescent rebellion against authority starts. Antisocial behaviour can lead to exclusion. New relationships with both sexes. Influenced by media messages. Perceptions of gender roles tend to be stereotyped. Friendships increasingly important especially in Y9. Many have paid jobs and have savings accounts.	Shift of interest from family to the group, which provides a backdrop to developing self-identity. Causes intense self-preoccupation which can be interpreted as selfishness. Crime rate peaks for girls. Homophobic bullying.
– emotional	Developing sense of self and gender identity. Becoming more independent. A range of egocentric behaviours shown. Understand simple cause and effect of behaviour. Unacceptable/antisocial behaviour seen in the context of powerful infantile emotions still dominating.	Need a language of feelings through which social skills can be developed. Possible mood swings. Defiant and difficult tendencies.	Interest in the range of sexualities – developing own sexual identity. Volatile adolescent emotions. Capable of abstract thinking. Understanding of moral reasoning. Move towards independence from parents. Relatively high incidence of attempted suicide. Bullying an issue in Y8. Peer pressure highest in Y9.	Pressures: social, sexual, academic, relationship can cause depression – increase in teenage suicide rate. A high proportion have at least one personal worry. Parental values and support continue to be important to the adolescent.
School Career	Starting full-time school can cause stress. Beginning to apply past learning to new situations. Eager to take responsibility in simple ways. Developing awareness of and need to care for the environment.	Exposed to more complex learning and more formal teaching and learning practices. Preparing for SATs and secondary school. Growing awareness of potential career opportunities.	Change from primary to secondary school – need to feel settled and cared for in the new environment – bullying is an issue. Making choices for KS4 courses. Starting to think about the future KS3 SATS.	Future plans are important – what to do post 16. Examinations, coursework and balancing part-time jobs can cause pressures and stress. Work experience takes place.
Health Career	Accidents still a hazard. Need to be aware of dangers and how to cope with them – including personal safety. Hygiene procedures established – washing hands, cleaning teeth.	Developing interest in sexuality and human reproduction. High accident rate – on cycles. Significant number do not wear safety cycle helmets. Experimentation with smoking starts. Relatively high incidence of deaths due to solvent abuse. Increasing knowledge of drugs. Boys developing strong interest in computers.	Road accidents prevalent at the KS2–3 change. Pressure from friends to conform in smoking, drinking, trying drugs etc. Girls more likely to smoke than boys. Excessive use of over the counter drugs. Exposure to illegal drugs at 13–14 years. A minority of pupils sexually active. Downward trend in the number of parents who talk with their children about sexual issues.	Risk-taking is an important part of teenage development. Health behaviour is often associated with peer group norms – smoking habits become regular for girls, drinking for boys. Eating patterns may change – 'snacking' contributes to obesity. Experimentation with drugs especially cannabis. Alcohol consumption is linked to motorcycle accidents and unintended pregnancy. Coming to terms with a sexually active body – many become sexually active during this period; masturbation is common. Have sufficient knowledge about mechanics of sex and contraception – want a greater emphasis on relationships and social skills. Insecure knowledge about HIV transmission. Lack of knowledge about local contraceptive advice and support agencies.

Step 1b: Identify existing curriculum opportunities for personal and social development

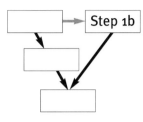

PASSPORT encompasses the whole curriculum, including designated PSE/PSHE courses, subjects and other activities.

It builds on the **Breadth of opportunities** identified in the PSHE framework, and will help schools to identify and analyse these experiences to bring coherence to planning and provision.

PSHE Framework: Breadth of opportunities

During the key stage, pupils should be taught knowledge, skills and understanding through opportunities to:

a) take responsibility
b) feel positive about themselves
c) participate
d) make real choices and decisions
e) meet and work with people
f) develop relationships
g) consider social and moral dilemmas
h) ask for help/find information/provide advice
i) prepare for change

From the National Curriculum Frameworks for PSHE and citizenship

Examples of activities in three schools illustrate the range of such opportunities.

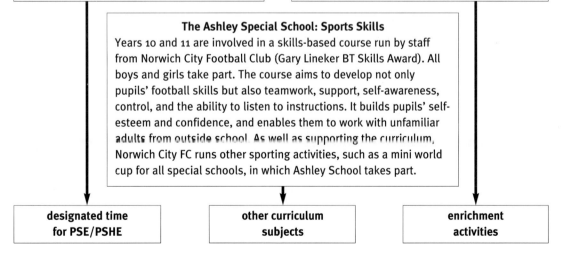

Christ Church School: Circle Time

In this 20 minute weekly circle time session, 23 reception class pupils sat in a large circle with the teacher and classroom assistant. They participated in the following sequence of activities:

- Song: 'This is circle time'.
- 'There's an empty chair next to me and I'd like .... to sit next to me because.........'

About five pupils took turns to choose someone to sit next to them.

- Round: I am wonderful!
- Closing with a song and a smile.

The teacher is working specifically to raise the self-esteem of many pupils. They are learning to recognise feelings and to think about how other people feel.

Broadlands School: Understanding Industry Day

This day at the start of the Summer Term is designed to prepare Year 10 for work experience in June. It has national sponsorship and involves two industrialists and two teachers with each group of 20, randomly mixed, students. The groups rotate around four activity-based workshops:

- health and safety in the workplace;
- essential skills for business (key skills); including a group problem-solving scenario;
- preparing for interview using the Record of Achievement and undergoing a mock interview;
- personnel issues e.g. what is expected of employees.

Pupils emerge from the day more confident about work experience, and more aware of the value of teamwork.

The Ashley Special School: Sports Skills

Years 10 and 11 are involved in a skills-based course run by staff from Norwich City Football Club (Gary Lineker BT Skills Award). All boys and girls take part. The course aims to develop not only pupils' football skills but also teamwork, support, self-awareness, control, and the ability to listen to instructions. It builds pupils' self-esteem and confidence, and enables them to work with unfamiliar adults from outside school. As well as supporting the curriculum, Norwich City FC runs other sporting activities, such as a mini world cup for all special schools, in which Ashley School takes part.

designated time for PSE/PSHE	other curriculum subjects	enrichment activities

These three broadly different curriculum contexts offer potential for PSD
= combination model of delivery

How to identify opportunities for personal and social development across the curriculum

It is the task of the year or key stage co-ordinators/heads of year to review the curriculum to identify the significant opportunities which can promote personal and social development for their particular year/ key stage.

The co-ordinator will need to use different sources of information for each of the three curriculum contexts.

Curriculum context	Where?	Who?	
DESIGNATED TIME e.g. circle time PSE course tutorial programme careers programme	Schemes of work for – PSHE – Citizenship – Health education – Careers education – Tutorial programme – Circle time	PSHE, citizenship and health education co-ordinators Year/KS co-ordinators Heads of year Careers co-ordinators	To contribute to the curriculum for PSD, an opportunity must: • be for **all** pupils in the year group • be designed to provide **at least one** of the key opportunities (opposite page) • offer pupils **time for reflection** on their personal and social learning
+			
Specific opportunities in existing curriculum **SUBJECTS** e.g. Jump Rope in PE sex education in science	Subject schemes of work Literacy and numeracy programmes	Subject co-ordinators Heads of department Literacy and numeracy co-ordinators	
+			
Curriculum enrichment/ off-timetable/extended **ACTIVITIES** e.g. Health Week Insight to Industry Day School Council	School calendar Assembly programme	Co-ordinators of specific events Assembly co-ordinator	

Although **every** curriculum opportunity has the potential for personal and social development, schools may wish to select particular experiences for which there will be more detailed planning and reflection.

When identifying the opportunities the following questions need to be addressed:
- What particular kinds of opportunity does the subject/activity offer to promote personal and social development? (See Breadth of opportunities on page 19 – there may be more than one).
- Are all pupils involved in the activity?
- Does planning for the subject/activity include personal and social development?
- Do pupils reflect on what they have learned about themselves?
- In relation to personal and social development, how does the subject/activity focus on what pupils: are able to do (skills); know and understand (knowledge); and have thought about (attitudes and values)?
- Does the subject/activity offer the opportunity to teach, practise or assess personal and social skills?

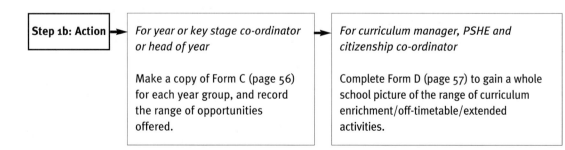

Step 1b: Action

For year or key stage co-ordinator or head of year

Make a copy of Form C (page 56) for each year group, and record the range of opportunities offered.

For curriculum manager, PSHE and citizenship co-ordinator

Complete Form D (page 57) to gain a whole school picture of the range of curriculum enrichment/off-timetable/extended activities.

Opportunities for PSD during the school career

It is useful to build up an overview of the main events during the school year which have potential for promoting the pupils' personal and social development. This shows the spread of events across the age groups and the range of different activities. It highlights the people who come into school to work with pupils in each year group and points up any imbalance in opportunities between years. An example from one school is shown in Fig. 5. A blank matrix is included on page 57 (Form D).

Planned Opportunities for PERSONAL AND SOCIAL DEVELOPMENT in this academic year

Year	Residential	Theatre in Education	School Council	Visits	Visitors	Artists-in-Residence	Equal Opps	Junior Citizenship	Work Experience		Special events may include
7 MLD	1 WEEK OF DAILY ACTIVITIES (WITHIN NHANTS)	FRENCH THEATRE GROUP.	1 CLASS REP. MEETINGS 1-2 PER TERM	CHURCHES OF DIFFERENT DENOMINATIONS PETERBOROUGH CATHEDRAL LONDON MOSQUE	SCHOOL DENTIST WOOD GREEN ANIMAL SHELTER DOG WARDEN GOODWILL	VISITING AUTHOR 'BOOK' DAY FAIR WEEK'	✓	THEMES x 2 WEEKS SCHOOL POLICE OFFICER	—	JEANS FOR GENES DAY.	Work-based problems Industry Days Careers Conventions
8 MLD	YORKSHIRE FARM (4 DAYS)	"	"	ICE SKATING PETERBOROUGH BRASS RUBBING CENTRE CAMBRIDGE	CHILDRENS VILLAGE (INDIA) BEN STOCKHAM (GHANA TRIP) CHILD LINE ROMAN CENTURIAN			ST. BARNABUS CHURCH WELLINGB' HINDU TEMPLE CHILDREN SOC. BLUE PETER APPEAL.			Health weeks Peer mediation Peer counselling
9 MLD	OVERNIGHT STAY IN SCHOOL	"	"	2 WORK PLACEMENTS	DOG DRUG SEARCH. DISABLED ATHLETE CAREERS OFFICER		OPTIONS x 2	"	CAREERS LESSON 1 HR PER WK INTERVIEW INPUT FROM ADVISOR.		Reception Duty Enterprise days Mock Interviews
10 MLD	ACTIVITY WEEK 1 NIGHT IN TENT	—	"	N.C.I.P. WORK SHADOW LIBRARY	" + N.C.I.P. SPEAKERS		OPTIONS CAREERS.	INTO THE COMMUNITY PLACEMENT	2 DAY WORK SHADOW	KS4 CHARITY AFTERNOON	Careers Interviews Environment Projects Also see page 45
11 MLD			"	NAT HISTORY MUSEUM.	FROM: TESCOS MACDONALDS		OPTIONS CAREERS.	'CHILDRENS RIGHT' LINKS WITH SERVICE SIX	1 DAY A WEEK — 2 WK BLOCK (2 NOV + MAY) EXTENDED WORK PLACEMENT		
KS3/4 SLD	1 WEEK OF VISITS LINKED TO YEARS TOPICS.	FRENCH THEATRE GROUP.	"	CHRIST THE KING CHURCH KETTERING. LIBRARY. VARIOUS SHOPS/CAFÉS ON WEEKLY BASIS.	DENTAL HYGENIST. SCHOOL NURSE. REV. NATLDE. ENGLISH SINFONIA (1 DAY).		— ✓	WEEKS THEME —	YEAR 9 CAREERS INTERVIEW IND. LIFESKILLS PROG. PREP FOR LEAVING SCHOOL		

Fig. 5   Friars Special School

PASSPORT 'Guarantees'

Key opportunities for personal and social development which pupils might expect during their school career:

- to take part in activities which are designed to promote success and receive special recognition for achievements;
- to have access to a range of options and to exercise some choice between them e.g. choices about their future, and in relation to their health;
- to meet and work with adults other than teachers, including members of the community, professionals and business people;
- to interact and work with a wide range of people who are different from themselves;
- to organise a project or event in co-operation with others;
- to take responsibility for themselves individually and in a group with support and access to resources;
- to take responsibility for others: visitors, younger pupils, people with special needs;
- to be trained to provide support and advice for their peers and for younger pupils;
- to take on some responsible role in school; and to exercise leadership and initiative and to receive feedback on their performance;

- to take part in the decision-making process of the school;
- to be involved in developing and implementing the school's policies and strategies which aim to improve its ethos e.g. anti-bullying;
- to influence the school as a health-promoting community;
- to perform for an audience, individually or as part of a group;
- to take part in adventurous and challenging activities in a supportive environment;
- to have a residential experience;
- to take part in community service;
- to be involved in an environmental project;
- to gain experience and understanding of the world of work;
- to participate in debate or action about a local, national or global issue;
- to learn from experience in simulated situations e.g. theatre-in-education, Junior Citizenship;
- to have time for reflection and preparation for change.

Based on the idea of an education service's 'guarantees' to its pupils, developed by Professor Tim Brighouse, CEO, Birmingham LEA.

Step 2: Identify what pupils should learn

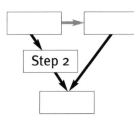

This step will identify more precisely what the pupils need to learn from the curriculum for PSD during the year.

Planning the curriculum using the PASSPORT Learning Outcomes will ensure a coherent programme suited to individual schools' and their pupils. **The PASSPORT Learning Outcomes for PSHE and citizenship at key stages 1–4 can be found on pages 24–31.**

The learning outcomes:

- describe a basic entitlement for pupils to a curriculum for personal and social development;

- have been cross-referenced to the framework for PSHE and citizenship at key stages 1 and 2; the framework for PSHE at key stages 3 and 4; and the programmes of study for citizenship at key stages 3 and 4. (*See National Curriculum Handbooks for Teachers, QCA 1999.*)

- include additional elements of the following which relate to pupils' personal and social development: sex and relationships education; education for sustainable development; careers education; education for parenthood; education for financial capability. (*See page 11 for relevant publications.*)

- are framed in terms of **skills, knowledge and understanding, attitudes and values;**

- in some instances, incorporate aspects of more than one category, e.g. 'recognising risk situations' is a skill requiring some basic knowledge;

- are not intended to be prescriptive: the outcomes achieved at each key stage build on learning at the previous key stage. Schools, particularly special schools, will be able to select the learning outcomes appropriate to the level of understanding and ability of their pupils, regardless of key stage;

- are not intended to be used to measure, in any formal way, pupils' attainment against stated expectations at the end of each key stage. They will, however, help teachers to monitor the quality and scope of the wider PSHE and citizenship curriculum by the end of each key stage; and to consider which aspects of pupils' learning could usefully be assessed and reported on, and the best way to do this.

The PASSPORT Framework states in general terms what pupils can be taught. Each school should write its own specific learning outcomes. For example, both health issues and risks will vary from school to school, and different classes may need to focus on particular communication skills.

Personal and social development at each key stage
The focus of the curriculum for PSD will shift as the pupils grow and develop. As pupils mature, different issues become significant and they become susceptible to different influences. Opportunities are presented during each key stage which can help pupils develop in a balanced way consistent with their age.

The focus for programmes of PSD during each key stage is summarised opposite (page 23).

Step 2: Action

For curriculum manager, PSHE and citizenship co-ordinator

i) Photocopy Form E (pages 58 and 59) one for each year group.

See completed examples on page 33.

ii) Using the information from Form B, complete column 1 of Form E. Column 1 should state the priorities for PSD.

iii) Complete column 2 of Form E using the PASSPORT Learning Outcomes, identifying, for each priority, what pupils should:
- be able to do (skills)
- know and understand (knowledge)
- have thought about (attitudes and values)

Programmes of PSD at key stage 1 should

- build on the 'Early Goals' for personal development in the early years of schooling as a basis for all other learning;

- emphasise the development of basic rules and skills for keeping safe, help pupils to manage their behaviour and begin to show that they can take some practical responsibility for themselves;

- help pupils to learn the social skills they will need to become part of the classroom community;

- adopt structured activities such as circle time to allow pupils to practise essential skills and to develop positive attitudes to being a member of the class;

- help pupils to become less egocentric and more socially competent and motivated by the end of the key stage.

Programmes of PSD at key stage 2 should

- make use of this, the longest of the key stages, to provide opportunities for extended/class/year projects, particularly on local, national or global issues;

- support pupils as they start to question themselves at the beginning of the process of developing into young adults;

- provide more frequent contact with adults from outside the school offering new opportunities and challenges;

- produce pupils who are confident and independent learners, able to organise themselves, manage projects and take responsibility;

- ensure that before they leave primary school pupils are:
  – prepared for the impact of puberty before it begins;
  – confident about the transition to secondary school.

Focus for programmes of PSD at each key stage

Programmes of PSD at key stage 3 should

- acknowledge and build on the levels of confidence, independence and skill developed in the primary school, and maintain pupils' zest and motivation through the whole key stage;

- attend to pupils' anxieties about friendships and bullying through induction programmes;

- provide opportunities to reassure pupils that physical and emotional changes are normal;

- introduce pupils to the benefits that community involvement can provide for themselves and others, through tutor group activities, charitable projects and community service;

- develop pupils' career awareness as a preparation for selecting key stage 4 courses;

- enhance the curriculum by providing enriching and developmental experiences as pupils mature, through special events and days off-timetable.

Programmes of PSD at key stage 4 should

- use the relatively short period of five and a half terms to enable pupils to apply the skills, knowledge and experiences they have acquired so far and take responsibility in the school and the wider community;

- focus on preparation for work and adult life, creating opportunities for pupils to perform new and more adult roles in the real world;

- help pupils to know themselves sufficiently well and to be sufficiently well informed as to be able to make appropriate decisions;

- provide opportunities for pupils to demonstrate that they can take responsibility for themselves and their learning, and set targets and plan to meet them;

- recognise pupils' desire to talk about changing relationships and to clarify their opinions and attitudes with their peers and with informed adults;

- help pupils to present themselves confidently and provide opportunities for them to represent the school to visitors and at outside events.

LEARNING OUTCOMES – KEY STAGE 1

OPPORTUNITIES TO ENABLE PUPILS TO:	SKILLS	KNOWLEDGE	ATTITUDES & VALUES
1 Develop confidence and responsibility and make the most of their abilities	1 Recognise and name feelings, including those associated with change e.g. new family member. 2 Begin to manage feelings positively and effectively. 3 Ask for and give permission. 4 Recognise what they are good at from what others tell them. 5 Express positive qualities about themselves. 6 Respond with increasing confidence to new people and situations. 7 Set simple targets for themselves. 8 Perform simple tasks independently.	1 Know their personal likes and dislikes. 2 Understand ideas of good and bad, and right and wrong. 3 Know some of the things which can cause different emotions. 4 Know what they are good at. 5 Know that it is alright to make mistakes.	1 Believe in fairness for all. 2 Develop confidence when expressing opinions about things that matter to them. 3 Think about what responsibility means. 4 Recognise their uniqueness, feel good about themselves and be proud of their achievements. 5 Want to do well, and make the most of opportunities and talents. 6 Persevere and overcome difficulties.
2 Prepare to play an active role as citizens	1 Listen to the teacher and to a friend. 2 Hold the the attention of a listener. 3 Ask simple questions of a range of adults. 4 Take part in discussions about matters relating to their lives e.g. the school environment, bullying. 5 Recognise and make safe choices based on right and wrong/good or bad. 6 Agree rules for the group/classroom. 7 Show some responsibility for self and others in and out of school e.g. classroom, playground, school visits. 8 Observe surroundings and suggest how they might help to improve them. 9 Work together as a group or class on a project about a social or environmental issue.	1 Know the choices open to them e.g. in food, games and activities. 2 Know the school and classroom rules and why they are necessary. 3 Know how to behave in different situations. 4 Understand that other people, pets and plants have needs. 5 Know that all people have the same basic needs, and the difference between needs and wants. 6 Know the different groups to which they belong e.g. family, friends, school. 7 Know the world immediately around them including local services e.g. library, leisure centre, museum etc. 8 Know about the jobs of adults in the classroom, school and around them. 9 Know what improves and harms their local environment and how they can look after it. 10 Know about shops, services and advertising, and what they do for us; know that they have to pay for what they buy.	1 Be aware of their right to decide. 2 Think about what is important to them in making choices. 3 Think about their responsibilities to their friends, class, family. 4 Care about people who have unmet needs. 5 Consider the value of being part of different groups and communities e.g. a family and local community. 6 Appreciate and want to care for their environment: classroom, school grounds, local area. 7 Value natural resources and understand that they are limited. 8 Respect their own and other people's property, personal and public. 9 Show concern for the impact of their actions on others and the environment. 10 Want to participate, make a difference. 11 Think about how money can be spent other than on themselves.

3 Develop a healthy, safer lifestyle

1 Make simple choices e.g. between foods, activities.
2 Maintain personal hygiene e.g. washing, teeth cleaning, toilet routines.
3 Recognise potential risks to safety of self and others from people, situations and in the environment.
4 Say 'no' when subject to pressure/something feels wrong.
5 Ask for help from adults.
6 Follow simple safety rules and instructions.

1 Know what keeps them healthy: food, exercise, rest.
2 Know that some people need drugs to live a normal life and that some drugs can prevent the development of diseases e.g. immunisation.
3 Understand the concept of growing from young to old and that they are growing and changing.
4 Know the correct names for the external parts of the body including the sexual parts.
5 Know what is safe to put into/onto the body and that all substances can be harmful if not used properly.
6 Know that all medicines are drugs but not all drugs are medicines.
7 Know places that are safe, where to get help and the people in their community who can help them.
8 Know the rules for keeping safe at home and at school e.g. roads, fire, water, household substances, 'Stranger, Danger', knives, sun screens, medicines, tablets, and solvents.
9 Know when to keep a secret and when to tell.
10 Know that they have rights over their own bodies.

1 Be proud of their body, enjoy what it can do and treat it with respect.
2 Think about why it is important to know what they are eating.
3 Want to be healthy and clean.
4 Think about why they need to take care and be safe in what they do.
5 Care about keeping themselves and others safe.

4 Develop good relationships and respect the differences between people

1 Voice differences of opinion sensitively and courteously; say sorry, thank you.
2 Recognise ways in which their own choices and behaviour affect others.
3 Co-operate with others in work and play; share; take turns.
4 Show respect by listening to what other people say.
5 Recognise worth in others, and say why someone is special to them.
6 Make new friends; cope with losing friends.
7 Help to care for pets and plants.

1 Know that different types of family have common features and functions.
2 Know that there are similarities and differences between people: gender, appearance, abilities, families, cultural background etc.
3 Understand that boys and girls can both do the same tasks and enjoy the same things; but that stories and the television sometimes say that boys do this and girls do that.
4 Know that people have things in common but that every individual is unique.
5 Understand how to be a friend and that friendships can change.
6 Know the people who look after them and their different roles and responsibilities.
7 Know what bullying is and what to do if they experience or see bullying.
8 Understand that there is a difference between accidental and purposeful hurting.

1 Consider the value of being a friend and having friends.
2 Be proud of who they are and understand that difference does not mean better or worse.
3 Value other people's achievements.
4 Begin to accept everyone as an individual.
5 Respect others' needs, feelings and opinions.
6 Be willing to care for others.
7 Value the ways in which their family is special.
8 Think about what trust and reliability mean.
9 Think about why bullying is unacceptable.

LEARNING OUTCOMES – KEY STAGE 2

OPPORTUNITIES TO ENABLE PUPILS TO:	SKILLS	KNOWLEDGE	ATTITUDES & VALUES
1 Develop confidence and responsibility and make the most of their abilities	1 Ask questions and talk confidently with adults and peers about their thoughts and feelings. 2 Record information about current interests and choices they will have to make in the future. 3 Express positive things about themselves and others. 4 Use simple vocabulary for describing personal effectiveness and setting personal goals. 5 Prepare for and manage the change to secondary school. 6 Show reliance in finishing tasks. 7 Recognise the need to ask for support sometimes, and whom to ask and how. 8 Recognise and respond to a variety of emotions in themselves and others, such as jealousy, anger, excitement. Be able to express feelings in different ways and recognise the impact on others. 9 Be able to express feelings in different ways and recognise the impact on others. 10 Transfer a skill learned in one situation to another context. 11 Interview adults to find out about job roles or tasks.	1 Know what is special about them: abilities, interests, strengths and weaknesses. 2 Know that puberty brings about changes in emotions. 3 Know ways of coping with difficult emotions, fears and worries. 4 Know the range of jobs and work roles carried out by people they know and what they like/dislike about those jobs. 5 Know the range of knowledge, skills and personal qualities required for different types of work. 6 Know how their strengths can help a group to perform a task. 7 Know about the basic ways of saving money.	1 Enjoy life at school, acting confidently and appropriately. 2 Have realistic aspirations when target setting. 3 Look forward confidently to the transition to secondary school. 4 Value opportunities for new experiences in and out of school, including opportunities to meet adults other than teachers. 5 Appreciate the importance of taking responsibility for themselves and their behaviour. 6 Respect other people's work and career choices. 7 Consider why saving money is important. 8 Consider how different values influence how they spend money e.g. pocket money.
2 Prepare to play an active role as citizens	1 Use different ways to communicate and express personal and group views about social and environmental issues. 2 Contribute to decision-making in a small group e.g. setting rules for the class and the school. 3 Use local environmentally sustaining facilities e.g. paper/can banks. 4 Put themselves in someone else's shoes e.g. people who are less fortunate than them. 5 Resolve problems/conflicts democratically through discussion, using different approaches to decision-making and reaching consensus. 6 Make decisions about use of scarce resources; evaluate information about priorities for spending: personal, community, environment. 7 Make informed decisions on how to allocate fund-raising money. 8 Recognise when choices are affected by the media and other influences.	1 Understand why school rules are made and the consequences of breaking them; relate this to simple knowledge about the law and understand that rules and laws are designed to protect. 2 Know the variety of communities to which they simultaneously belong: family, school, local, national, European and worldwide, and the interdependence of individuals, groups and communities. 3 Understand that rights bring responsibilities at home, at school and in the community. 4 Have a simple understanding of democratic processes and how they can be applied in school and government. 5 Know about local voluntary and community groups and what they do. 6 Understand that groups have different views: peers, parents, teachers etc. and people of different faiths and cultures. 7 Know about the different national, regional, religious and ethnic groups and which of them are reflected in their school community. 8 Understand how their spending decisions affect them personally, the local economy, the environment and people in other parts of the world. 9 Understand how they and others can cause changes for better or for worse especially in their immediate surroundings and also in their wider community. 10 Know how advertising influences supply and demand.	1 Consider why a sense of fair play is necessary in their dealings with their peers and others. 2 Consider why it is wrong for children to be bullied or abused by other children or adults. 3 Show interest in their local community and show a wider sense of social responsibility. 4 Appreciate home, school and community values. 5 Develop a concern for people and communities where human needs are not met, and consider the effect of inequalities which exist between people in different countries. 6 Be honest. 7 Consider the possible effects of lifestyle on health. 8 Value their own identity and background and those of others. 9 Appreciate the positive impact of human activity on plants, animals and the environment and value the aesthetic qualities of their surroundings.

3 Develop a healthy, safer lifestyle

Skills

1. Choose healthy options in relation to food, exercise, rest etc.
2. Manage hygiene procedures: e.g. food safety, menstruation.
3. Discuss and ask questions about changing bodily needs.
4. Decide who has access to their bodies.
5. Recognise risk in different situations and make judgements about behaviour and decisions about personal safety.
6. Recognise unwanted influence and pressure from friends particularly in relation to smoking; and exercise some basic techniques for resisting.
7. Identify hazards to health and safety at home, at school and in the environment.

Knowledge

1. Know some of the options open to them in developing a healthy lifestyle now and in the future.
2. Know what makes them feel happy and positive about life; the influence of exercise, leisure, relationships on mental health.
3. Know bacteria and viruses affect health and how transmission may be reduced by using simple, safe routines.
4. Know about different cultural practices in health and hygiene.
5. Know how changes at puberty affect body hygiene.
6. Know that body changes are a preparation for sexual maturity, and understand the processes of conception and birth.
7. Know about the range of human variation, understand what is meant by 'normality' and know that differences between people can be caused by their genes and environment.
8. Know about a range of legal drugs encountered in everyday life including over-the-counter drugs such as aspirin, drugs prescribed as medicines, as well as tea, coffee, tobacco and alcohol, and have some understanding of their effects and their associated risks.
9. Know that some substances are illegal and have some understanding of their effects and the associated risks.
10. Understand that pressure to take harmful or illegal substances may come from people they know such as friends, relatives and neighbours.
11. Know school rules/safety rules relating to medicines, alcohol, tobacco, solvents and illegal drugs; know that discarded syringes and needles can be dangerous.
12. Know basic emergency aid procedures and where to get help in different situations.

Attitudes

1. Respect their own and others' bodies.
2. Consider the value of keeping healthy and different attitudes to health and illness.
3. Accept responsibility for personal cleanliness.
4. Consider the important and beneficial role which drugs have played in society as well as the costs to society of drug misuse.
5. Explore attitudes and beliefs about different drugs and the people who may use or misuse them; be able to recognise stereotypes.
6. Recognise that some role models for young people take drugs e.g. in sports, and explore feelings about them.
7. Develop a positive approach and self-motivation towards personal safety and risk-taking.

4 Develop good relationships and respect the differences between people

Skills

1. Recognise their own and other people's feelings.
2. Recognise that actions have consequences for themselves and others.
3. Put themselves into their parents' shoes.
4. Show care for others as well as for themselves.
5. Treat animals with care and sensitivity.
6. Initiate friendships.
7. Develop skills needed for relationships e.g. listening, supporting, showing care.
8. Respond assertively to teasing and bullying.
9. Recognise and challenge stereotypes.
10. Demonstrate tolerance and respect for others.

Knowledge

1. Know what we do that makes each other happy, sad and cross, and what helps and what hinders friendships.
2. Know that people live their lives in different ways and that different cultures may have different life patterns.
3. Know that people's responses to ideas and events may be determined by age, religion, culture.
4. Develop understanding of different types of relationship including marriage, and know that there are many different patterns of friendship.
5. Understand what families are and what members expect of each other.
6. Know how to deal with friendship problems.
7. Understand more about the changes that take place in human life – parenthood, bereavement, making new relationships.
8. Know about bullying, why it happens, its effects on people, how to deal with it and how to stop it happening.
9. Understand how media messages affect attitudes and can cause inequality of opportunity.
10. Know that human sexuality is expressed in different ways, understand what it means and have some words to describe it.
11. Know sources of help, including helplines, when facing problems.

Attitudes

1. Respect other people's feelings, decisions, rights and bodies.
2. Value diversity of lifestyles, and the choices made within them.
3. Consider why honesty, loyalty, understanding and respect are important in relationships.
4. Appreciate different ways of loving and the importance of love in relationships.
5. Appreciate that similarities and differences between people are the result of many factors.
6. Consider their developing responsibilities at school, with friends and within the family.

LEARNING OUTCOMES – KEY STAGE 3

OPPORTUNITIES TO ENABLE PUPILS TO:	SKILLS	KNOWLEDGE	ATTITUDES & VALUES
PSHE **1 Develop confidence and responsibility and make the most of their abilities**	1 Reflect on strengths, achievements, areas for development and preferred ways of learning in all areas of their lives. 2 Give and receive constructive feedback. 3 Recognise that failure can help them to learn. 4 Recognise and manage strong feelings in different situations, including loss and change. 5 Assess personal strengths and set realistic targets for development at KS2–3 transition and throughout the key stage. 6 Research information independently especially in relation to career plans. 7 Manage time and learning effectively. 8 Make informed choices for KS4.	1 Know that there are different sexual orientations as they develop a sense of sexual identity. 2 Understand what makes them feel good and bad, and that how they see themselves affects self-confidence and behaviour. 3 Know how others see them. 4 Know the stages of emotions associated with loss and change caused by death, divorce and separation, and new family members. 5 Know the broad job categories, aptitudes and basic qualifications needed for them; relate these to subject choices for KS4. 6 Understand that jobs and work patterns change and know some of the factors which affect this. 7 Know where to access information about jobs, learning and leisure. 8 Understand what influences our behaviour e.g. how we spend/save money; staying out late.	1 Enjoy the new opportunities of the secondary school. 2 Feel motivated about and value learning. 3 Enjoy public recognition of their achievements. 4 Value their own and others' achievements. 5 Be positive when offered new opportunities. 6 Be realistic and positive in their aspirations in relation to their KS4 choices and future careers. 7 Consider the values which guide their spending decisions.
2 Develop a healthy, safer lifestyle	1 Look after their bodies at puberty especially personal hygiene. 2 Recognise signs of personal stress and use strategies to manage it. 3 Assess potential risks in relation to alcohol, smoking and sexual behaviour. 4 Make safe choices e.g. on the roads; in the water; and with fireworks. 5 Demonstrate ways of resisting pressure which threatens safety. 6 Be assertive in the face of pressure to do wrong. 7 Gain access to help in and out of school. 8 Follow instructions and administer simple emergency aid procedures.	1 Understand how the physical and emotional changes that take place at puberty affect them, and that there is a range of physical development which is normal. 2 Know what they need to keep healthy especially during puberty. 3 Know how the media influence attitudes to health and health behaviour. 4 Know how a balance of work and leisure, and positive relationships can promote mental health. 5 Know the basic facts and laws about illegal substances and the dangers of misusing prescribed drugs. 6 Know school rules and procedures for drug-related incidents. 7 Know about human reproduction, contraception, safe sexual practices, and the risks of early sexual activity. 8 Know about HIV transmission and other sexually transmitted infections (STIs) and the associated high-risk behaviours. 9 Know the safe levels for sunbathing and drinking alcohol. 10 Know the organisations, local and national, which can offer help and support.	1 Feel positive about entering adulthood. 2 Be realistic about body image. 3 Consider the benefits of a healthy lifestyle. 4 Consider what respect for their bodies means. 5 Consider the personal costs of risk-taking, including the effects on other people's lives. 6 Consider the consequences of ignoring the law.
3 Develop good relationships and respect the differences between people	1 Show concern for and defend others by challenging prejudice and discrimination. 2 Put themselves into other people's shoes, e.g. their parents/carers, friends, teachers. 3 Make and keep friends of the same and opposite sex. 4 Make positive statements to friends and family.	1 Understand what prejudice and discrimination mean, and the effects in relation to difference – culture, gender, sexuality, disability, age etc. 2 Understand the different forms of bullying – how it feels, why people do it, the school's code of practice and what is expected of individuals.	1 Support strongly the unacceptability of bullying. 2 Consider personal feelings about people who are different. 3 Consider the benefits and costs of trusting other people. 4 Value their friends. 5 Consider at what age young people may be ready for sexual activity.

5 Seek help and support by themselves from outside agencies.
6 Talk with, and listen to, peers and adults.
7 Negotiate within relationships e.g. with friends, parents/carers.
8 Resolve conflicts without anyone losing face: at home and with friends.
9 Resist pressure from others to behave in a way which would make them feel uncomfortable.
10 Recognise when others need help and support them.
11 Communicate confidently with adult visitors to the school.

3 Know that there are different cultural norms in society today in sexual relationships and family life.
4 Know that there is a range of sexual lifestyles.
5 Understand the pressures on relationships and the changing nature of relationships with friends and family.
6 Understand how marriage and other stable relationships support children as they grow.
7 Understand the roles and feelings of parents/carers.
8 Know how personal actions can affect others' lives and what influences their own behaviour.

6 Respect the fact that families are different.
7 Respect the fact that parents have feelings and concerns about their children.
8 Consider the responsibilities of parenthood and the value of family life.
9 Have concern for friends' and others' well-being.
10 Consider feelings about different sexual relationships.
11 Think about how far they can, and should, be responsible for others.

CITIZENSHIP

1 Know and understand about becoming informed citizens

1 Recognise bias and misrepresentation in the media and advertising.
2 Assess their own lifestyle and their contribution to sustainability

1 Understand what independence, rights and responsibilities mean to them.
2 Know the main laws which affect them and their families; understand the consequences of breaking the law and the impact it has on themselves and the community.
3 Know the law for this age group especially in relation to part-time jobs.
4 Understand the structures of central and local government, what they do, and how they are linked to each other.
5 Understand what democracy means and relate it to how decisions are made in school and in government.
6 Understand that using a vote enables them to take part in decision-making.
7 Know about the voluntary groups which contribute to their local community.
8 Understand the interrelationships between the community, the economy and the environment.
9 Understand the concept of 'Fair Trade'.
10 Understand the role of the EU, the Commonwealth and the UN and the relevance to their lives e.g. the UN 'Rights of the Child'.

1 Respect and value the environment and other living things.
2 Respect evidence in relation to social and environmental issues.
3 Believe that they have some personal responsibility for the environment.
4 Consider:
– the concept of fairness and justice through the school rules and sanctions;
– the contribution that cultural diversity makes to society;
– how much independence they should have at this age;
– the benefits of taking responsibility in school or the community;
– why behaviour codes are necessary;
– whether it is irresponsible to break the law;
– the impact of the unequal distribution of wealth;
– the benefits of working collaboratively, and independently;
– the importance of sustainability for the future;
– ethical and social dilemmas arising from the scientific and experimental use of animals.
– the personal benefits, and the benefits to others, of active community participation;
– entitlement to equality.

2 Develop skills of enquiry and communication

1 Express rational arguments having researched social, moral and environmental issues.
2 Present opinions, values and beliefs confidently, clearly and concisely.
3 Be able to detect bias and omission in others' arguments.
4 Listen to, summarise and be able to add to an argument during class or group discussion.

1 Know about local social and environmental issues on which they could have some impact.

3 Develop skills of participation and responsible action

1 Empathise with others and express opinions that are not their own.
2 Participate in group activities for the local environment or community.
3 Negotiate and contribute to making decisions as part of a productive group.
4 Make compromises to reach consensus.
5 Apply personal strengths to group and individual tasks.
6 See a task through to completion.
7 Reflect on learning from experience, individually and as a group member.

1 Understand the processes involved in working together.

LEARNING OUTCOMES – KEY STAGE 4

OPPORTUNITIES TO ENABLE PUPILS TO:	SKILLS	KNOWLEDGE	ATTITUDES & VALUES
PSHE **1 Develop confidence and responsibility and make the most of their abilities**	1 Review transition from KS3–4, assess personal qualities, skills and achievements honestly. 2 Set future personal goals by reflecting on the results of past decisions. 3 Demonstrate and record Key Skills on work experience. 4 Present themselves confidently on a range of occasions. 5 Manage different roles confidently. 6 Recognise and manage negative feedback. 7 Manage failure and learn from experience. 8 Recognise and manage positive influences and negative pressures e.g. support from teachers and stress caused by examinations. 9 Budget for living independently. 10 Manage money sensibly through saving accounts and know how to use cash dispensers and banks. 11 Negotiate with adults about post-16 options and make realistic choices. 12 Analyse strengths in learning, plan to develop skills and extend knowledge further. 13 Organise work and meet deadlines in coursework and revision. 14 Gain access to information independently.	1 Have a sense of their own identity and know the roles they have and want to have. 2 Understand the need to be adaptable. 3 Understand what expectations people in the workplace will have of them. 4 See themselves through other people's eyes. 5 Know about different ways of saving money. 6 Have an in-depth understanding of areas of occupational interest which could lead to a future career. 7 Understand all the options post-16: higher education and training as well as employment. 8 Know how further education and training can improve job prospects, job satisfaction and mobility in the labour market. 9 Understand the links between the UK and the EC in relation to work opportunities. 10 Know how changing work patterns can affect post-16 choices. 11 Know how the Careers Services can help them to choose progression routes.	1 Have a sense of purpose about their future. 2 Be positive about the control they have over their own behaviour. 3 Be positive about personal achievement. 4 Want to get the best out of school life. 5 Value learning for its own sake. 6 Consider the importance of success on self-esteem. 7 Consider the benefits of accepting advice from others. 8 Consider whether personal values and attitudes have to be the same as other people's. 9 Consider how the media influence public opinion and promote different lifestyles. 10 Be positive about contributing to the country's workforce. 11 Consider the importance of life-long learning in society today.
2 Develop a healthy, safer lifestyle	1 Recognise alternatives and long- and short-term consequences when making decisions. 2 Counter and challenge unwanted pressure. 3 Recognise the initial signs and symptoms of stress in themselves and others, and have strategies for preventing and reducing it. 4 Assess risks related to sexual activity, drug misuse, drinking alcohol, sunbathing etc. 5 Set and keep safe levels when drinking alcohol. 6 Seek confidential health advice from advisory and support agencies confidently. 7 Know how to find information related to health, e.g. local leisure and fitness facilities. 8 Administer emergency aid.	1 Understand signs, causes and treatment for depression and know where to get help. 2 Understand the links between eating disorders, unhealthy eating and low self-image. 3 Understand consumer aspects of food hygiene and the food labelling system. 4 Know the specific dangers of misusing alcohol and drugs in relation to: driving, pregnancy and sexually transmitted infections (STIs). 5 Know the demographic trends in relation to STIs including HIV. 6 Understand how the different forms of contraception work, to inform future choices. 7 Know what is meant by safe and safer sex. 8 Know about health and safety in the workplace.	1 Consider benefits of leisure for health and work. 2 Consider personal attitudes to mental illness. 3 Respect the body. 4 Consider the benefits and costs of using recreational drugs. 5 Consider the costs of early sexual activity. 6 Consider their attitudes towards drug users and suppliers. 7 Consider their attitude to the law in relation to drugs, including licensing and retailing. 8 Consider the advantages and disadvantages of different forms of contraception in terms of personal preference and social implications.
3 Develop good relationships and respect the differences between people	1 Recognise when others are taking advantage and resist it. 2 Give and receive support. 3 Challenge offending or unfair behaviour in others. 4 Work with a range of people different from themselves. 5 Talk about relationships, including sexual relationships, and feelings to a parent/carer and friend/partner. 6 Detect emotional nuances, from tone of voice and body language.	1 Understand that there is diversity within different ethnic groups. 2 Understand the power dynamics of prejudice. 3 Be aware of the effects of homophobic and racial bullying. 4 Understand what exploitation in relationships means. 5 Understand that different communities have their own codes of behaviour. 6 Know more about the diversity of sexual orientation. 7 Know the stages of child development.	1 Consider personal assumptions about people who are different. 2 Respect different ways of life, beliefs and opinions. 3 Be willing to live and work alongside people different from themselves. 4 Respect that people have different needs in relationships. 5 Consider how feeling good about themselves affects their relationships.

6 Consider the costs and benefits of being independent of parents.
7 Consider the benefits and costs of a stable marriage or partnership in bringing up children.
8 Consider why loving and caring are important in relationships.
9 Consider what factors contribute to the quality of family life.
10 Consider how having a baby changes a relationship.

7 Manage changing relationships using a range of strategies.
8 Resolve disagreements peacefully.
9 Negotiate with parents to gain increasing independence.
10 Work well with adults on work experience, and community service.

8 Understand the responsibilities of parents, step-parents and grandparents and the roles they can play in nurturing children.
9 Understand the needs of babies, and of old and disabled people.
10 Understand the impact of separation, divorce and bereavement on families.
11 Know the statutory and voluntary organisations which offer support in human relationships.

CITIZENSHIP

1 Know and understand about becoming informed citizens

1 Have concern for human rights.
2 Understand that growing up involves both freedom and responsibility.
3 Recognise the responsibility involved in being an elected representative.
4 Be willing to play a full role as a citizen in the electoral process.
5 Be compassionate for humanity.
6 Make a commitment to being an active member of the local and school community.
7 Consider:
– attitudes to the law in relation to the age of consent;
– a range of ethical issues e.g. of having a baby or an abortion if unable to support it/against one's religion;
– whether right and wrong are always clear cut;
– how far they can be responsible for their own behaviour;
– what constitutes 'value for money';
– the effects of wasting money;
– why consumer rights are important;
– whether we have a duty to contribute to sustaining the environment, locally and globally;
– a range of ethical issues about the use of animals.

1 Consult people about their views and wishes.
2 Interpret media messages.

1 Understand legal rights and responsibilities in relation to this age group.
2 Know how the Youth Justice system works.
3 Know what human rights mean in relation to action in a global context.
4 Know how the UK developed its diverse national identity.
5 Know how parliament and government make laws in order to understand the role they can play locally.
6 Understand how business and financial organisations affect their daily lives.
7 Understand the tension between having a free press and its power to inform national opinion.
8 Know legislation and rights in relation to employment.
9 Understand equal opportunities legislation in relation to employment and bullying in the workplace.
10 Understand the ways in which individuals and organisations can contribute to sustainable development locally and globally, and know about Agenda 21.
11 Understand how far their responsibilities extend in contributing to the life of the school.
12 Understand that the basic needs of a large part of the world's population go unmet.
13 Understand that being part of the EU provides opportunities and brings responsibilities.

2 Develop skills of enquiry and communication

1 Understand the ethical and legal issues around economic, social and environmental matters.

1 Research and analyse information about a social/moral issue, and show awareness of use and abuse of statistics.
2 Present ideas to a variety of audiences, large and small.
3 Argue a case around moral and ethical issues confidently.
4 Form balanced and reasoned arguments about social and environmental issues for class debate.

3 Develop skills of participation and responsible action

1 Understand the elements of effective group work and the concept of 'group life'.

1 Empathise with, and express, how it might feel to be a person living in an economically developing country.
2 Be an active member of the local and school community.
3 Communicate effectively as an ambassador for the school.
4 Work effectively alone and as part of a team.
5 Take responsibility and/or initiative in a group task.
6 Reflect on their contribution to a group task – what they have learned and what they have given.

Step 3: Plan the curriculum provision for pupils' personal and social development

The final stage in the planning process assigns learning outcomes to particular curriculum contexts. It should be carried out by the curriculum manager responsible for the programme for personal and social development, including PSHE and citizenship, in consultation with all staff contributing to the curriculum for PSD.

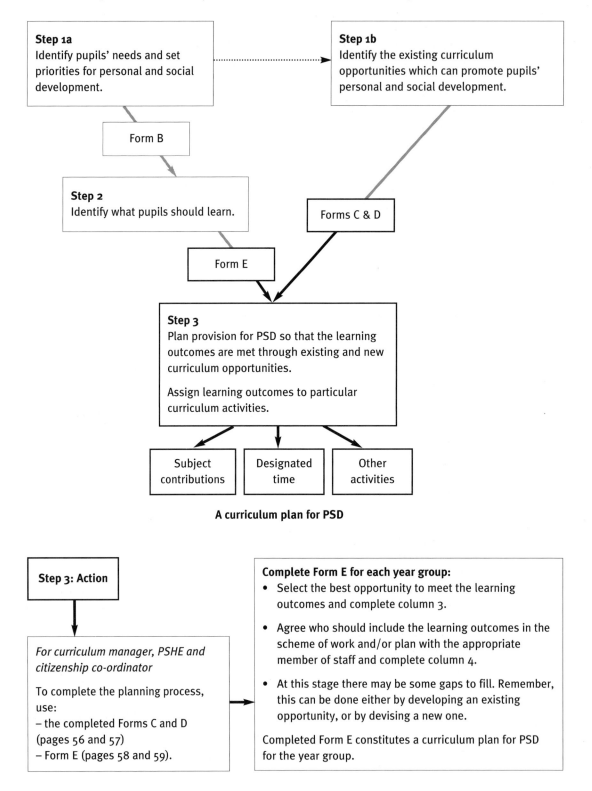

A curriculum plan for PSD

Step 3: Action

For curriculum manager, PSHE and citizenship co-ordinator

To complete the planning process, use:
– the completed Forms C and D (pages 56 and 57)
– Form E (pages 58 and 59).

Complete Form E for each year group:
- Select the best opportunity to meet the learning outcomes and complete column 3.

- Agree who should include the learning outcomes in the scheme of work and/or plan with the appropriate member of staff and complete column 4.

- At this stage there may be some gaps to fill. Remember, this can be done either by developing an existing opportunity, or by devising a new one.

Completed Form E constitutes a curriculum plan for PSD for the year group.

When all the forms are completed for each year group, schools will have a whole curriculum plan for personal and social development.

Form E: Plan the curriculum for PSD

Example – Year 6

PSD priority	Learning outcomes	Curriculum context	Responsibility
1 Preparation for puberty	*Skills:* Ask adults questions of concern; Ask an adult for help; Manage personal hygiene e.g. menstruation. *Knowledge and understanding:* Know how and why both boys' and girls' bodies change at puberty; Understand the basic processes involved in conception and birth; Understand that pubertal changes start at different times, and that they eventually happen to everyone. *Attitudes and values:* Accept responsibility for an increased need for personal cleanliness at puberty; Feel good about becoming an adult.	Circle time Session with school nurse (girls only) Science Science Circle time	Class teacher School nurse Class teacher School nurse Class teacher

Example – Year 8

PSD priority	Learning outcomes	Curriculum context	Responsibility
1 Assertiveness skills to resist pressure if offered drugs	*Skills:* Behave assertively when under pressure; Make safe choices; Ask for help. *Knowledge and understanding:* The difference between a healthy and unhealthy lifestyle; The basic facts and laws relating to substance misuse; The risks involved to self and others from substance misuse; Where to go for help in and out of school. *Attitudes and values:* About their own behaviour; Personal costs of risk-taking behaviour; Responsibility to others; Consequences of breaking school rules and the law.	Health Study Day PSE follow-up Health Study Day Science Science PSE PSE follow-up and assembly	PSE teacher Science teacher Police liaison PSE teacher PSE teacher Year head Police liaison

The next step – from plan into practice

The curriculum plan, as represented by Form E, can be used for the following tasks:

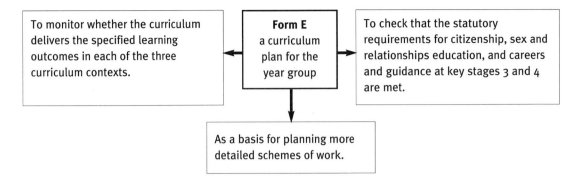

To monitor whether the curriculum delivers the specified learning outcomes in each of the three curriculum contexts.

Form E
a curriculum plan for the year group

To check that the statutory requirements for citizenship, sex and relationships education, and careers and guidance at key stages 3 and 4 are met.

As a basis for planning more detailed schemes of work.

Preparing schemes of work for PSD

Form E represents a curriculum plan; it is not a scheme of work. However, it will become a key reference document when schemes of work are created or updated. Where a teacher has been nominated on Form E to deliver specific PSD learning outcomes within a subject or activity, these should be reflected in an amended scheme of work, a copy of which should be given to the co-ordinator.

The co-ordinator should keep a record of the following schemes of work:

Designated time for PSE/PSHE:	Schemes of work for each unit.
Subjects:	Extracts from subject schemes of work showing PSD outcomes, and mode of assessment.
Other activities:	A plan, equivalent to a scheme of work, describing what the pupils will do, what they should learn and how it will be assessed.

A scheme of work for PSD

A scheme of work should answer the questions: who? what? when? where? and how?
Each school has its own format in which to display this information.

Who is it for?	Pupils in a year group or class.
What is it about?	Aims of the activity or unit of work. – what do the pupils do? – what are the key opportunities provided? – what are the pupils expected to learn (learning outcomes)?
When is it taught?	Term; duration of the activity or unit.
Where is it taught?	Curriculum context: PSE designated course; subject; other activity.
How is it taught?	How is the unit of work or activity delivered? – what teaching methods are used? – what resources are needed: people? materials? – how will the pupils' learning and achievement be assessed? – who will assess the pupils? pupils themselves; peers; teachers; others.

The case studies on pages 47–53, provided by the PASSPORT pilot schools from all over England, set out many of the details useful in a scheme of work. A blank form for a case study is given on page 54.

3 Implementing a curriculum for PSD using the PASSPORT Framework

The PASSPORT Framework is intended to help schools provide a broad, coherent and developmental curriculum for PSD which includes, but goes beyond, any designated courses for PSE/PSHE. How it is planned, organised, co-ordinated, managed, monitored and evaluated are important issues which are addressed in this section. It looks at:

1 Managing the curriculum for PSD
2 The organisation of the curriculum for PSD
3 Teaching to promote personal and social development
4 Teaching methods for different purposes
5 Confidentiality and handling sensitive and controversial issues
6 Assessing, recording, and reporting personal and social development
7 Monitoring and evaluating the curriculum for PSD
8 The focus for staff development

1 Managing the curriculum for PSD

a) The role of the curriculum manager as PSD co-ordinator

As all curriculum activities have the potential to promote the pupils' personal and social development, all staff in the school have some contribution to make to this. Responsibility for a whole curriculum approach to PSD should be held by a senior member of staff responsible for curriculum management.

The curriculum manager will need to:
- raise awareness amongst all staff of their contribution to the pupils' personal and social development and agree the overall aims, objectives and priorities;
- establish a shared view of best practice to which all pupils are entitled;
- lead PSD policy development;
- agree the main priorities for the pupils' personal and social development in each year group with year teams and identify the major opportunities for meeting these priorities across the curriculum;
- provide appropriate support and training for staff;
- monitor and evaluate the programme, including the use of outside agencies, and pupils' responses to the programme;
- carry out a continuous process of review and development of the programme as part of the annual cycle of school improvement;
- support and co-ordinate staff responsible for particular aspects of the programme such as PSE/PSHE and citizenship courses, PSD elements of other subjects, circle time, work experience, residential trips and so on.

b) Management style and school ethos

A curriculum for PSD needs to be underpinned by a management style, ethos, organisation and policies which accord value and respect to all members of the school community, as described on page 12. Pupil involvement in the school's decision-making processes, particularly through school councils, is a trend which can be expected to grow with the introduction of active citizenship into the curriculum.

2 The organisation of the curriculum for PSD

a) The curriculum for PSD: a combined model of delivery

The curriculum for PSD is spread across three main curriculum contexts: designated PSE/PSHE/circle time; other subjects; and enrichment activities (see pages 19–20). This combined model of delivery is not only the most effective way of providing the breadth of opportunities needed to meet pupils' entitlement to personal and social development, but is also an efficient way of making provision in an already crowded curriculum.

In most primary and special schools, PSD can be readily included in a coherent way across the curriculum. The increasing use of circle time activities provides further opportunity to focus on personal and social learning.

In secondary schools, PSE/PSHE courses taught by tutors and/or by a specialist team are usually part of designated time in the curriculum. However, PSD cannot be covered effectively by courses alone and opportunities should be sought through other subjects and activities across the curriculum.

b) The time allocated to designated PSE/PSHE and citizenship

This should be timetabled at least weekly. Reliance on occasional off-timetable experiences, such as Health Days, prevents curriculum continuity. A notional minimal time allocation for the designated time should be 20–30 minutes for primary-age pupils and an hour for secondary pupils, which should be a continuous period so that learning can be consolidated. The practice of 20 minute 'slots' in secondary schools during tutor time results in fragmentation and militates against progression.

Citizenship will be introduced as a new national curriculum subject in key stages 3 and 4 in September 2002, with some new statutory requirements. As PASSPORT demonstrates, there are many common elements in the PSHE and citizenship frameworks. Using PASSPORT for curriculum development will ensure coherence. It is unnecessary, therefore, to introduce separate citizenship lessons to replace PSE/PSHE. However, there are some aspects of citizenship, concerned with political literacy, which may fall outside the curriculum for PSD. In due course schools will need to check that all outstanding statutory requirements are met. If these elements of citizenship are to be taught during designated PSE/PSHE time, more time will be needed to do justice to both PSHE and citizenship.

c) A specialist team for PSD

In primary schools all teachers make a major contribution to the curriculum for PSD. At the same time, some may specialise in particular aspects such as sex and relationships or drugs education and provide support to other staff.

In secondary schools, roles are more differentiated. It is important to ensure that teachers can contribute to the curriculum for PSD in the way most suited to their role and their level of training and experience.

Form tutors are often responsible for the PSE/PSHE course, but evidence from Ofsted and others underlines the importance of training and support if form tutors are to be motivated and pupils are to benefit fully. Tutors often have a good relationship with their forms; they know the pupils well and can help them to review their personal and social development and set personal goals. Tutor groups frequently have responsibility for organising school events, such as assemblies, which provide excellent opportunities for the pupils to develop and demonstrate their skills and confidence.

Evidence shows that in secondary schools the quality of PSE/PSHE courses is enhanced when they are taught by a specialist team of trained teachers. The advantages of this arrangement are: teachers have commitment and expertise; PSE is perceived as having greater status with pupils; PSE has recognised curriculum status with other subjects; specialised training opportunities and resources are made available.

All teachers need to understand how they can contribute to their pupils' personal and social development. They need particular skills, which will require opportunities for training. These issues are considered more fully in 'The focus for staff development' on page 44.

3 Teaching to promote personal and social development

The curriculum for PSD encompasses the full range of subjects and other activities, and involves many different staff. The potential to foster personal and social development is best realised where:

a the teacher acts as facilitator;

b pupils learn, practise and demonstrate personal and social skills;

c pupils are actively involved in, and take responsibility for, their learning;

d pupils reflect on their learning and plan the next step.

a) The teacher* acts as facilitator   (*teacher/tutor/visitor/employer etc.)

The facilitative role involves being supportive, enabling pupils to take some control over their own learning, and acknowledging the value of the pupils' experiences and contributions. The teacher needs to plan and prepare carefully, both for lessons and for other more open-ended or off-timetable activities, so that there are clearly identified learning outcomes and time for reflection on personal and social learning.

The teacher needs to organise and manage the learning effectively. This entails:

- arranging the room to create a flexible space for movement, different activities and multiple groups;
- creating a positive climate to promote the development of supportive relationships and trust;
- setting ground rules for working together to encourage pupils to be responsible for their behaviour;
- varying the types of working groups, such as friendship, interest and random groups;
- managing discussion, encouraging all pupils to contribute without the teacher dominating.

b) Pupils learn, practise and demonstrate personal and social skills

Personal and social development is enhanced if the school actively teaches the skills which will enable pupils to participate fully in the experiences open to them. The essential skills include personal skills (managing feelings and reflecting on personal experience), communication skills, decision-making skills, practical skills and skills for working with others. These overlap significantly with the Key Skills increasingly valued by employers and seen as part of the profile of graduates from further and higher education. They can be developed from key stage 1. Once pupils have acquired the skills, they can demonstrate them in, for example, group tasks, discussions, projects and presentations, and possibly have them accredited (see page 40).

c) Pupils are actively involved in, and take responsibility for, their learning

There exists a wide repertoire of active teaching methods which enable pupils to develop personally and socially. These methods have in common:

- a focus on active learning and pupil participation;
- placing a value on the pupils' experiences and contributions;
- teacher acting as a facilitator.

Traditionally many PSE teachers have relied on worksheets and videos. While they have a place, if used exclusively they are unlikely to promote personal and social development. Teachers should select the most appropriate method to meet the aims of their lesson or activity. A list of purposes for which different methods may be used is given on page 38.

d) Pupils reflect on their learning and plan the next step

Learning from experience necessarily involves reflection. Every activity should include a planned and timed period for reflection. Reflection should never be omitted.

Following an activity, pupils can share reactions and start to make sense of the experience in relation to themselves and others. They can identify what went well, what went wrong, and why. From this they can draw conclusions about their own strengths and weaknesses and those of the group as a preparation for self and peer-assessment and target setting.

Reflection can be structured around the following questions:

- What happened?
- How did I feel when experiencing the event/exercise?
- What did I learn from the experience/exercise?
- How can I apply what I've learned?

4 Teaching methods for different purposes

Good teaching relies on using appropriate methods for the aim of the lesson or unit of work. Teachers therefore need a repertoire of flexible, active learning methods.

- **Starting and ending**

Whole group activities mark the beginning and ending of sessions, encourage participation, and emphasise the importance of working together. It is good practice to start in a circle, and share the aims of the session with the pupils. Coming back together at the end can bring a session to a purposeful conclusion.

- **Climate building and ground rules**

In a positive climate of trust and support, pupils share their experiences, listen carefully to one another and acknowledge one another's feelings. Activities encouraging mixing with their peers set the tone for what will follow. When pupils work together, it is essential to agree ground rules for how they should treat each other.

- **Agenda setting**

Pupils should be consulted about the content of lessons and invited to set the agenda for future work. Useful trigger materials include uncaptioned pictures or the Draw and Write technique (page 16). Pupil surveys may also be used, and action research projects allow pupils to exercise choice and responsibility over their work.

- **Working together**

Small group work helps pupils to take responsibility for tasks and learn about how groups function. Group work skills, such as listening, letting others contribute, negotiation and reflection, need to be taught. Group-forming activities mix pupils in new ways, and pupils benefit from this variety.

- **Values clarification**

A number of methods enable pupils to compare their views with others and to appreciate the spread of opinion in a group. For example, pupils can form an attitude continuum according to how strongly they hold a particular attitude or actually show where they stand on controversial issues (standpoint-taking).

- **Information gathering and sharing**

Information can be gathered from different sources and shared in an active way, which is especially useful when a variety of primary sources such as pamphlets, book or newspaper extracts, video clips or ICT must be studied. Small groups can scan one source each and then share the main points with others.

- **Consensus building**

Activities which require pupils to reach agreement about a view or course of action help them to consider ideas and concepts in a progressive way, and to refine their views and negotiate until consensus is reached. Pupils learn to listen, interpret ideas, clarify language, justify different positions, compromise and take collective ownership of ideas and decisions. Card games that involve prioritising can help pupils practise this.

- **Problem solving**

Everyday problem solving is a process that entails clarifying the problem, generating different solutions through brainstorming, evaluating and selecting the best solution. Pupils need to be aware of different ways to make decisions and the skills that are essential to the process.

- **Understanding another point of view**

Acquiring empathy is an essential part of personal and social development. Done well, role play is an effective technique to help pupils put themselves in someone else's shoes. Visitors to the classroom also help pupils to gain insight into how other people think and feel.

- **Working with feelings and imagination**

Around a circle, invite people to say in turn how they feel at a particular moment. Pupils need to know that they have the right to 'pass' when their turn comes. Difficult feelings can be written anonymously on slips of paper, collected and drawn out of a box to be discussed in the group. Guided fantasies can help groups to explore feelings in a personal and creative way.

- **Reflection, review and evaluation**

Reflection is the process of looking back over an activity (see page 37); review involves identifying what has been learnt and applying this understanding to future experience; evaluation enables a judgement to be made about the value of an experience to the individual and the group. Time should be set aside during and at the end of a session for the group to discuss what has happened. Ways of gauging the response to a session include evaluation voting, rounds, and writing short comments on graffiti sheets.

5 Confidentiality and handling sensitive and controversial issues

a) Confidentiality

Pupils occasionally make personal disclosures, either in class or to individual teachers. They may disclose that they are engaging in under-age sexual activity; that they, or friends or relatives, are using drugs; or that they have been abused. Teachers may come to possess sensitive information about pupils, some of it about illegal activity. All parties need to be clear about the rules of confidentiality which apply in these circumstances. A school policy about confidentiality will reassure teachers.

Relevant principles to consider

- A policy about confidentiality should provide guidance about who needs to know in particular instances. Information about pupils should not be passed on indiscriminately. The headteacher may wish to be informed in all or some circumstances; staff have a contractual obligation to comply.

- Teachers should not offer pupils or their parents unconditional confidentiality. Information about behaviour likely to cause harm to the pupil or to others must be passed to the appropriate agency.

- Teachers should make it clear to pupils that although most information can be kept confidential, some may need to be passed on in the young person's best interest. However, the pupil will know when this has to happen, what will be done with the information and who will have access to it.

- In the case of illegal activity, action should be taken in the best interests of the pupil. This does not necessarily involve informing the police. Teachers are not obliged to inform the police about illegal drug activity, for example. The school's police liaison officer will provide specific guidance.

- Teachers are not obliged to pass on information about pupils to their parents, although where the teacher believes the pupil to be at moral or physical risk, or in breach of the law, they must ensure that the pupil is aware of the risks and encourage them to seek support from their parents.

- Where outside agencies and others provide support for the PSE programme, they must be made aware of, and abide by, the policy about disclosures and confidentiality. However, they may also have a role in providing advice and support directly to pupils. The boundary between these two roles must be agreed with the school and the distinction, in terms of the right to confidentiality, be made clear to pupils.

- Some people are bound by their own professional codes of confidentiality. For example, the school nurse is bound by the medical code of confidentiality in his or her work with children and young people. Pupils who seek help from teachers about their personal health e.g. contraception or pregnancy, can be referred to the school nurse or their family doctor.

- In lessons, teachers should establish from the beginning that it is inappropriate to disclose personal information. Ground rules, which ensure pupils agree not to pressure one another to answer questions about their own experiences, also apply to staff.

b) Handling sensitive and controversial issues

Sensitive and controversial issues are certain to arise in PSE/PSHE and citizenship teaching; in fact, the aim of the programme may be to enable pupils to address these issues directly and to develop the skills of reasoned argument. Sex education, religion and politics are examples of topics which concern values and beliefs and which may, therefore, arouse strong feelings. Their place in the curriculum is regulated by law. Other issues likely to be sensitive or controversial include family lifestyles and values, law and order, environmental issues, bullying and bereavement.

Teachers should:
- ensure pupils establish ground rules about how they will behave towards each other and how the issue will be dealt with;
- judge when to allow pupils to discuss issues on their own in small groups and when to join in and offer support;
- ensure that pupils are clear about the difference between fact, opinion and belief, and that they have access to balanced information and views against which they can then clarify their own opinions and views, including contributions made by visitors to the classroom;
- decide how far they are prepared to express their own views, bearing in mind that they are in an influential position and that they have to work within the school's values framework;
- provide appropriate support after a session for any pupil who may be troubled by an issue raised.

6 Assessing, recording and reporting personal and social development

The PASSPORT Framework for PSD is a planning tool rather than a set of criteria against which pupils can be assessed. However, by detailing the skills and knowledge which pupils should have the opportunity to learn, pupils and teachers can develop shared criteria useful for setting personal goals and agreeing strategies to reach them, and against which assessment of progress and recording achievement can take place.

a) Assessing

Assessment is as central to personal and social development as it is to any other learning process. Baseline assessment, with regular reflection on personal experiences, provides information which can be indicative of pupils' progress and achievement.

The central role of self-assessment

The individual's feelings and responses must always be respected. In the past, schools have been reluctant to introduce assessment in PSE in case pupils are deemed to 'fail as people'. Sensitive teachers understand that some aspects of personal and social development are not linear; for example, self-esteem can rise and fall through the influence of events at any stage of life.

- Any judgement about self-worth has to be made by the individual. It should be their decision whether they share it with others.
- Unlike knowledge and skills, it is inappropriate to assess pupils' values. However, pupils should be encouraged to reflect on how their personal values relate to those of the school and society, and on the consequences of challenging these values.

Assessment, therefore, should allow the learner to:

- pose the questions;
- make the judgement in the light of the evidence of his/her current strengths and needs;
- reconsider and plan in terms of his/her growth and development.

This will have a positive impact on a pupil's self-awareness and self-esteem.

Self-assessment can be influenced by the views of others. Information from a range of sources will help pupils to see themselves through the eyes of other people.

What can be assessed?

- Factual knowledge and understanding: knowledge of facts (the effects of drugs, why hygiene is important, where support and help can be found) is the least difficult aspect of personal and social development to assess. Non-threatening approaches using quizzes, word searches, and games work best. Understanding and being able to apply knowledge may be observed and assessed in real or simulated experiences, e.g. during the planning of projects or in role play;
- Personal and social skills: schools must ensure that pupils have had opportunities to learn and practise these. They can then be assessed in real or simulated activities.

Who can be involved in assessing skill level and progress?

- Individuals themselves, their peers and teachers;
- Adults from outside school, for example, employers can assess pupils' skills during work experience or when carrying out mock interviews. Junior Citizenship programmes enable younger pupils to practise and become proficient in a range of health and safety skills.

Opportunities to gain accreditation

- Schools have their own award systems for accrediting competencies;
- Local and national bodies, for example, ASDAN Youth Award and the Duke of Edinburgh Award Scheme offer awards that can supplement school initiatives;
- National standards for the Key Skills are built into a number of qualifications. GNVQs provide a nationally recognised framework for accrediting some aspects of personal and social skills.

b) Recording

Teachers, pupils and parents will want to know what progress is being made in personal and social development. The different activities which contribute to the curriculum for PSD will generate opportunities to record learning and progress in different ways. Pupil profiles and Records of Achievement can provide a summative picture of the pupil. Formative evidence can be recorded by pupils in a number of ways.

<table>
<tr><td colspan="2">Evidence of personal and social learning and development can come from:</td></tr>
<tr><td>• Self-assessment</td><td>checklist
diary
display</td></tr>
<tr><td>• Peers</td><td>observation of role play
checklist
video/audio tapes
reflection in pairs or small groups</td></tr>
<tr><td>• The group</td><td>graffiti sheets
reflection on a group activity</td></tr>
<tr><td>• Teacher</td><td>checklist
observation of role play
written records</td></tr>
<tr><td>• Teacher
and pupil</td><td>one to one reflection based
on evidence</td></tr>
<tr><td>• Other adults</td><td>e.g. work experience report
Junior Citizenship awards</td></tr>
<tr><td>• Documentation</td><td>certificates of achievements</td></tr>
</table>

c) Setting personal goals and action plans

Pupils need a chance to reflect on what they have achieved as a result of all the different experiences which have had an impact on their personal and social learning. They can then identify areas for development. This process of personal goal setting and action planning is normally carried out in discussion with class teachers or, in secondary schools, with tutors and is essential to raising levels of achievement and encouraging pupils to take more responsibility for their own learning.

d) Reporting

Schools are required to keep records on all aspects of pupils' development, so it is appropriate for the pupils' annual school report to include a commentary on personal and social learning in the same manner as academic reporting. Teachers and tutors should negotiate statements from the earliest years, with pupils taking increasing responsibility for them as they become older. Pupils in key stages 3 and 4 will receive an annual report on citizenship.

7 Monitoring and evaluating the curriculum for PSD

The responsibility for monitoring and evaluating the curriculum for PSD lies at different levels within a school: – within classrooms;
  – with middle managers: subject and pastoral leaders;
  – with whole school leadership;
  – with parents, governors and in the wider school community.

The annual school development planning cycle is an essential tool to ensure entitlement to quality experiences which are needed to promote pupils' personal and social development and to raise standards of achievement. Monitoring and evaluation form part of this cycle.

a) PASSPORT and monitoring

> **MONITORING** is an ongoing process which ensures that the PSD programme is being effectively implemented.

The PASSPORT Framework identifies the learning opportunities and experiences which provide stimulus and context for personal and social development. The school should monitor both the extent to which a programme offers these opportunities as an entitlement to all pupils and the quality of the experiences available.

Form E (pages 58–9), when completed for each year group, provides a basis for monitoring provision.

Checklists
for: CLASSROOM TEACHERS
- Do lesson plans include learning outcomes for personal and social development?
- Do tasks engage pupils actively in their learning and provide opportunities to work with each other?
- Does planning meet the needs of all pupils?
- Are pupils given opportunities to reflect on their personal and social learning?
- Do you need help with clarifying the purpose of the work or teaching strategies?

for: YEAR AND KEY STAGE CO-ORDINATORS, HEADS OF YEAR, SUBJECT CO-ORDINATORS AND HEADS OF DEPARTMENT
- Are you clear what aspects of the PSD programme you are responsible for?
- How are you monitoring the curriculum experiences which contribute to pupils' personal and social development?
- Do schemes of work identify the core opportunities and experiences for promoting personal and social development with the intended learning outcomes?
- How are you monitoring teaching in relation to the strategies being used?
- How are pupils being given the opportunity to identify what they have learned, assess their progress and give and receive feedback?

for: CURRICULUM MANAGERS
- Do you have procedures for co-ordinating the planned programme of PSD?
- How are you monitoring the staff involved in the programme at middle management level?
- Is balanced use being made of specialist visitors and organisations?
- How are you monitoring the personal and social development which takes place as part of activities outside the classroom?
- How are you monitoring entitlement for all?
- How are you ensuring that the targets set in the school development plan are being implemented?
- Are you keeping staff and governors updated on progress?

b) PASSPORT and evaluation

> **EVALUATION** is the process which measures whether the programme is effective and worthwhile

The PASSPORT Framework identifies the potential outcomes of the pupils' personal and social learning. The extent to which these outcomes have been met, gauged from feedback from a variety of sources, notably the pupils themselves, will provide the basis for evaluating the PSD programme.

Checklists
for: CLASSROOM TEACHERS
> Evaluating a lesson and a unit of work
* Have you involved pupils in the evaluation?
* Were the aims and objectives met?
* What did pupils learn in terms of:
  new knowledge/concepts?
  new skills?
  attitudes and values?
* What went well?
* What will you change next time?

for: YEAR AND KEY STAGE CO-ORDINATORS, HEADS OF YEAR, SUBJECT CO-ORDINATORS AND HEADS OF DEPARTMENT
> Evaluating a unit of work and/or the PSD programme for the year group
* Have all the identified priorities been met by different aspects of the programme?
* Have you involved the appropriate people in the evaluation: pupils; tutors/subject teachers; other visitors who have contributed to the unit/programme?
* Have schemes of work sufficiently addressed the core elements needed to promote personal and social development, i.e. the learning opportunities and outcomes?
* What have been the highlights of the programme?
* What targets are needed for development and what actions need to be taken to achieve them?

for: CURRICULUM MANAGERS
> Evaluating the PSD programme as part of the annual review of the school development plan
* Has the evaluation considered the feedback from all the appropriate people: pupils; subject and pastoral leaders; parents; outside contributors to the programme?
* Does the policy and practice meet the overall aims and values statements?
* Does the programme reflect pupil-identified needs and any new priorities, locally and/or nationally determined?
* Are there sufficient planned opportunities across the curriculum for personal and social development to take place, including interacting with the community and learning from real life experiences?
* What has the school achieved over the past year in promoting pupils' personal and social development?
* What targets will further develop the PSD programme?
* What does the action plan imply for staff development and resources?

8 The focus for staff development

Training is the key to raising the quality of teaching and the status of the PSD curriculum in schools. By presenting a whole curriculum model as part of a whole school approach, both PASSPORT and the national frameworks for PSHE and citizenship identify not only the nature and quality of the experience to which pupils are entitled, but also the role of all teachers in its delivery. This last feature sets a standard against which schools can identify their staff development needs.

a) Training for all teachers

The whole curriculum approach implicit in the national frameworks for PSHE and citizenship means that all teachers will need to understand their contribution to its provision.

All teachers need to:
- understand their role in raising levels of self-awareness and self-esteem;
- know how to enable pupils to take more responsibility for their behaviour and learning;
- know how to act as facilitator, for example of class discussions and group projects;
- understand the importance of reflection and review to the learning process.

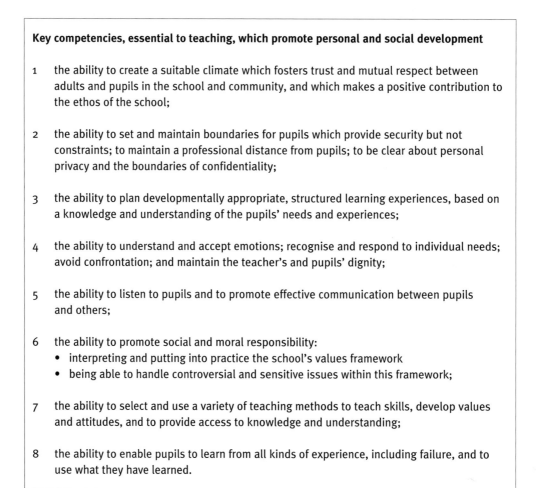

Key competencies, essential to teaching, which promote personal and social development

1   the ability to create a suitable climate which fosters trust and mutual respect between adults and pupils in the school and community, and which makes a positive contribution to the ethos of the school;

2   the ability to set and maintain boundaries for pupils which provide security but not constraints; to maintain a professional distance from pupils; to be clear about personal privacy and the boundaries of confidentiality;

3   the ability to plan developmentally appropriate, structured learning experiences, based on a knowledge and understanding of the pupils' needs and experiences;

4   the ability to understand and accept emotions; recognise and respond to individual needs; avoid confrontation; and maintain the teacher's and pupils' dignity;

5   the ability to listen to pupils and to promote effective communication between pupils and others;

6   the ability to promote social and moral responsibility:
- interpreting and putting into practice the school's values framework
- being able to handle controversial and sensitive issues within this framework;

7   the ability to select and use a variety of teaching methods to teach skills, develop values and attitudes, and to provide access to knowledge and understanding;

8   the ability to enable pupils to learn from all kinds of experience, including failure, and to use what they have learned.

b) Training for specialist teachers for PSHE and citizenship

Specialist training is necessary to teach some aspects of the curriculum for PSD. Training in sex and relationships and drugs education increases a teacher's confidence and leads to more effective teaching. Citizenship, sustainable development, financial capability, work-related and careers education will each require teachers to have some specialist knowledge and skills. Not all teachers need to be trained to this level; some teachers can take on the role of specialists as part of the overall team, and can teach these aspects, as well as provide support and resources for other members of staff.

Appendices

Introduction to the case studies

Learning opportunities which have the potential to promote personal and social development

The following pages contain examples of some of the opportunities that schools offer as part of their planned programme for personal and social development. They have been provided by the PASSPORT development and pilot schools from all over the country. Primary, secondary and special schools are represented, including some denominational schools. They provide examples from the three curriculum contexts i.e. designated time, other subjects and enrichment/off-timetable activities.

The case studies demonstrate:

- links with the national curriculum frameworks for PSHE and citizenship;
- evidence of planning – learning outcomes, and opportunities for pupils to reflect on their personal and social learning.

The examples can be used at staff meetings or for INSET to:

- introduce staff to the concept that personal and social development can be fostered across the whole curriculum and therefore is the responsibility of every teacher;
- help identify the range of opportunities which a school might already offer.

Writing a case study is a good way of analysing the learning opportunities and outcomes in existing curriculum activities and can be used to develop new ones.

Included is a blank form (Form A) which schools can use:

- as part of the consultation with staff at Steps 1b and 3 of the planning process;
- to monitor the effectiveness of the PSHE and citizenship provision;
- to report to the governors on the implementation of PSHE and citizenship;
- to gather a portfolio of evidence demonstrating the effectiveness of the school's curriculum for PSHE and citizenship for the National Healthy School Standard and for Ofsted inspections.

The examples are presented in two forms:

- using the case study format (Form A) – a detailed account of the activity, its links with the PSHE and citizenship frameworks and the learning pupils gained from it;
- a summary account, outlining the activity and the learning pupils gained from it.

Case studies: Key stages 1–4

Key stage 1

Corvedale C of E Aided School
Curriculum context: Literacy/PSE   **Activity:** Tackling bullying

After reading the book *Beryl's Box* by Lisa Taylor, the class of Year 1 and 2 children discussed the events in the story and identified feelings and possible responses. The children identified bullying as the main issue. They answered a questionnaire on what bullying is, where in school they feel safest and where it is most likely to happen, and who they would tell if it did. They were asked to draw a picture of a bully. The results of the questionnaire were tabulated in bar charts. The children developed an action plan and displayed it in the classroom. The work was then shared with the whole school at an assembly.

*This activity provides the **opportunities** for pupils to:*

a	take responsibility	√	f	develop relationships	
b	feel positive about themselves	√	g	consider social and moral dilemmas	√
c	participate	√	h	ask for help/find information/provide advice	√
d	make real choices and decisions	√	i	prepare for change	
e	meet and work with other people				

As a result of this activity the pupils

- are able to
  - recognise and name feelings;
  - recognise that one's actions have consequences for oneself and others;
  - listen, respond and contribute to a discussion;
  - identify causes and consequences;
  - co-operate, share, take turns;
  - recognise and be sensitive to the needs and feelings of others;
  - keep themselves safe;
  - use sources of help and guidance.

- know and understand
  - what a friend is and how to be a friend;
  - what bullying is and what to do if they experience it or see it;
  - when to keep a secret and when to tell.

- have thought about
  - the value of being a friend and having friends;
  - the concept of fairness for all;
  - their responsibility for themselves and others in different situations.

Questions for reflection: Based on the book *Beryl's Box*:
What do you think about the way the two main characters behaved to each other?
Why do you think they behaved that way?
What would it feel like if you were Beryl or Penelope?

Responses from pupils: Someone pushed me over, they bullied me.
When X called me names, I cried.
I don't like it when we go into the hall.
Someone who bullies you is always bigger than you.
I'd tell my mum or my teacher.
I'd tell my friend because she holds my hand.

This activity contributes to the following strands of the PSHE and Citizenship frameworks:

Personal development	√	Health and safety	√
Relationships	√	Active citizens	√

Key stages 1–2

Hopwood Primary School
Curriculum context: Whole school project   *Activity:* Safety week

---

The annual safety week has been held for the past five years. The whole week is devoted to specific safety issues and each year group follows its own set programme. In addition to this the co-ordinator organises visiting speakers, competitions, certificates, displays, leaflets and parents' sessions. The visitors' talks are followed up with carefully planned work by the teacher e.g. collaborative tasks, games, debates and problem-solving activities. Much of this work is of an active nature. The speakers themselves are carefully chosen for their ability to deliver the correct message to the appropriate age group. Topics have included: fire safety; first aid; cycling proficiency; road safety; home/school safety; medicines and all drugs; electrical safety; water safety; railway safety; building site safety; food safety; safety in the park; 'Crucial crew' for vandalism; decision-making and peer pressure.

The week enables pupils to consider a range of safety issues introduced by the outside speakers. They also learn new skills and try them out through role plays and activities such as designing leaflets and making presentations. They experience success through lots of opportunities to achieve.

Pupils also learn to recognise that their actions have a range of consequences; to listen to speakers and respond to what they have heard; to recognise risks and hazards, particularly of vandalism and litter; that the pressure to take harmful substances may come from people they know; and to keep themselves and others safe.

Responses from pupils: I enjoy meeting all the different visitors.
It's interesting so we are more likely to remember it and it will keep us safe.
You can learn a bit more each year.
I know I can cope when I get into a difficult situation.

Redhill Primary School
Curriculum context: Circle time/whole school   *Activity:* Big friends/little friends

---

When key stage 1 children enter the school they are all allocated a 'big friend'. The 'big friend' is a Year 5 child who is given responsibility for that child outside class time. The friends first meet the new pupils on their introductory visit the previous term. During subsequent visits, the big friends collect their charges for playtime and lunchtimes and look after them while eating and at play. They also meet the parents/carers of the little friends when they are invited in to lunch. This continues throughout their first weeks in school until the small children become independent. In circle time, the older pupils discuss other ways in which they can help their little friends and what their needs and fears may be.

This activity enables older pupils to put themselves into their little friends' shoes and imagine what they might feel like. They experience caring and being responsible for the wellbeing of a younger child.

They also learn to feel more positive and confident; to explain safety, hygiene and health issues relating to keeping safe at playtimes and cleaning out pets; and to appreciate that other people's needs and feelings must sometimes come first if they are responsible for them.

Responses from pupils:
How being a big friend has helped us:
I feel I have another friend who thinks I am special and kind.
Being a big friend has helped me by giving me responsibility.
It has helped me to learn how to look after other people even when I want to do something else.

Thinking about ways we have tried to build a friendship with our little friends:
Sometimes at 'privilege time' I would take her to our class and read her a story.
My little friend came to my house – it was the first time for her to go to someone's house.
I have made him confident enough to play with other young children – he no longer needs me any more.

Key stage 2

Flora McDonald Junior School
Curriculum context: Mathematics   ***Activity:*** Mental maths in the daily numeracy lesson

Year 3 pupils trialled the daily mathematics lesson and became very familiar and enthusiastic about the mental and oral elements. There was a wide diversity in the academic ability of the children in the class but they all took part in this session. On several occasions this overran the prescribed ten minutes due to the children's enthusiasm. Activities were varied and included chanting number sequences, with groups trying to improve precision, games with cards and dice and timed challenges for groups or individuals. There were no prizes but each group or individual worked hard to improve their previous score. This was the measure of their success and the children were all eager to demonstrate their skill. There was also a significant increase in these children's NFER test results for mathematics when tested at the beginning and end of the year.

*This activity provides the **opportunities** for pupils to:*

a	take responsibility		f	develop relationships	√
b	feel positive about themselves	√	g	consider social and moral dilemmas	
c	participate	√	h	ask for help/find information/provide advice	√
d	make real choices and decisions	√	i	prepare for change	
e	meet and work with other people				

As a result of this activity the pupils

- are able to
  - co-operate, share and take turns despite the fact that everyone wants a turn;
  - recognise and be sensitive to the feelings of pupils who find the tasks more difficult;
  - recognise worth in others especially those who are not normally the 'star' of the group;
  - cope with success and failure;
  - review progress, recognise personal achievements and set goals for improvement;
  - give and receive constructive feedback;
  - ask for help and support when forgetting facts;
  - use sources of help in reminding each other of little tips for completing a challenge.

- know and understand
  - what they were good at and when the task became too difficult for their friends;
  - that some slow readers are quick to recall number facts;
  - that some people struggle but will improve if supported, not ignored;
  - how to ask for support when challenges become too difficult.

- have thought about
  - volunteering for challenges as their confidence increased;
  - managing failure, and not letting it stop them trying again next day;
  - the meaning of friendship and loyalty;
  - the importance of fair play when working with their peers.

Questions for reflection: What do you enjoy about the mental mathematics sessions?
Why are the challenges exciting?
Have you learned anything besides maths?
Do you think your maths has improved?

Responses from pupils: It gives me a chance to understand what we're doing.
I like counting the seconds – sometimes people get it wrong and they need help.
No one looks silly when they get it wrong.
We learn how our friends think.
Very easy, we need bigger numbers.

This activity contributes to the following strands of the PSHE and Citizenship frameworks:

Personal development	√	Health and safety	√
Relationships	√	Active citizens	√

Key stage 2

Brownhill Special School
Curriculum context: Off-timetable   *Activity:* Lake District residential trip

A four day/three night excursion that offers a range of new, interesting, exciting and demanding experiences with links to humanities, science, English and PE, and helps to develop social skills. Flexible activities meet individual pupil's needs or difficulties, but generally include simple pond-canoeing, assault course, hill-walking, nature trail, mini-orienteering, swimming, and structured games.

This activity enables pupils to stay away in an unfamiliar and outdoor environment, often for the first time, to have lots of physical exercise, no TV or video games, fun and fresh air and to be together in a group. They apply skills and knowledge learned in school, such as following instructions and 'stranger, danger'; they work together in challenging situations; and look after, encourage, and show kindness to each other.

They also learn to deal with difficulties, challenges and fears; to feel comfortable about sharing feelings; to share responsibility with others in and around the hostel; to negotiate and reflect at the end of the day; and learn about safety rules on land and in the water. They learn about a town very different from their own; how to follow a map; develop interest in nature and how to care for the natural environment; to feel good about themselves and to value the team and their friendships.

Questions for reflection:	What was the best/most difficult/scariest/most enjoyable part of the trip?
	How can you be a good friend? A team mate?
Responses from pupils:	It was like a hotel, but there were no butlers!
	The mountains were massive and the lake was bigger than the sea!
	It was brilliant. I slept the whole night outside in a tent. It was tops!
	Billy helped me climb up onto the ledge. I was dead scared, but he waited for me and said 'Well done, mate'. I felt really good.
	Since the Lake District trip, I've made friends.

Key stage 3

Cullompton Community College
Curriculum context: Science   *Activity:* Introducing organs of the digestive system

Year 8 students use a cut-out diagram of the digestive system and follow a series of written instructions, with minimal help, to produce a colour-coded, labelled diagram with a key. This exercise follows a discussion, led by the students, on why digestion is necessary, why we eat, what happens to our food, why we feel hungry, etc. On completion of the cut-out diagram, the class reflects on their success in following the instructions and where improvements can be made. They also discuss the general structure and function of the digestive system and produce a table for the next lesson.

This activity helps pupils to co-operate on a group task whilst learning about digestion, and to identify ways in which they can improve their performance, individually and in a group, on future occasions.

They also learn to identify their weaknesses in following instructions; to talk, listen to and appreciate each other's ideas; to review progress and give and receive constructive feedback; to organise themselves to complete the task within the time limit; to share ideas effectively within the group; to understand the value of reviewing a task, when completed; and the value of breakfast as a source of energy.

Questions for reflection:	How did you manage your time in the session?
	How could you have improved it?
	How did you make sure that you followed the instructions effectively?
	How could you make this better next time?

Key stage 3

William Brookes School
Curriculum context: PSE   *Activity*: The Game of Living (and rules for playing)

PSE is being re-launched as a timetabled specialist subject. The Year 7 team decided to begin the year with a topic which would reinforce and complement the school's behaviour policy, while at the same time helping the new pupils to mix, get to know each other and work as a group. They developed a game-building exercise where classes, in small sub-groups, designed and made board games. Classes first thought about favourite games and why they were successful and enjoyable; fairness and clarity of rules emerged early on. They were then given the design brief and drafted ideas as homework. Back at school, the games were made up by groups of four chosen by the teacher. Subsequently, the games were exchanged, played, and a discussion and written evaluation followed. Lesson 3 examined the areas of life where safety, fairness, security and harmony, rules of one sort and another are needed, and ended with a brainstorm of rules which were most applicable to the classroom. These were then reduced to a core of ground rules for successful progress and learning for each class, and some classes came up with relevant slogans such as 'Share, Care, Be Fair!' Posters of the rules were produced for classroom display and they were exhibited as part of the school's open evening for incoming Year 6 pupils.

*This activity provides the **opportunities** for pupils to:*

a	take responsibility	√	f	develop relationships	√
b	feel positive about themselves	√	g	consider social and moral dilemmas	√
c	participate	√	h	ask for help/find information/provide advice	
d	make real choices and decisions	√	i	prepare for change	
e	meet and work with other people				

As a result of this activity the pupils have learnt the following:

Skills:	• reflecting on their own attitudes;
	• making new working relationships;
	• listening to, adapting, accepting, rejecting ideas and opinions from other students;
	• delivering constructive criticism to other groups in the class;
	• joint planning of games and co-operating in allotting tasks within the groups;
	• meeting deadlines for completion and testing.
Knowledge:	• understanding the elements which make a successful game;
	• knowing that all communal activities require agreed and fair rules;
	• knowing that successful learning depends on an agreed set of ground rules.
Attitudes and values:	• appreciating differing abilities, and viewpoints within groups;
	• appreciating the feelings of others;
	• examining their own values;
	• developing a common code of behaviour for their basic school community.
Questions for reflection:	What made the games we made and played good and less good?
	What situations in our lives need some kind of code or set of rules?
	What things do you think are important to make life in class happy and successful?
	Can we summarise these in a small number of agreed rules?
Responses from pupils:	The rules must be fair and must be obeyed by everyone equally.
	We need rules in sport and other games for our safety and to make it fair.
	People shouldn't call out or interrupt when someone else is speaking.
	Fairness, respect, honesty, sharing and supporting.

This activity contributes to the following strands of the PSHE and Citizenship frameworks:

Personal development	√	Health and safety	√
Relationships	√	Active citizens	√

Key stage 4

Batchwood Special School
Curriculum context: Careers   *Activity:* Opportunities Day

Twelve Hertfordshire special schools were invited to take part in a careers event with a range of business partners and the Hertfordshire Careers Service. The event, funded through Hertfordshire TEC, aimed to give young people an awareness of realistic job expectations, raise employer awareness that all young people can make a contribution and encourage more companies to provide job opportunities and work experience for young people with special needs. Pupils took part in a series of practical workshops which provided hands-on experience in retail, banking, hospitality and catering, newspapers, horticulture, facilities management, vehicle recovery and motoring services, and further education and training.

The activity allowed pupils to be in social settings with new people; to work co-operatively with others; to gain insight into coping with new people and experiences; to observe the health and safety rules; to explore potential career avenues and learn more about the steps they need to take to pursue them.

They also learn to cope with transitions, new situations, success and failure; to listen and respond to what they hear, build on one another's ideas, ask for help and support; to co-operate, share, take turns; to identify decisions to be made and problems to be solved; to recognise risks and hazards; to organise tasks and manage time; to have a more enhanced career awareness and awareness of the world of work; to appreciate the steps to be taken to enter a career; to understand different expectations and acceptable forms of behaviour in a work environment.

Responses from pupils: It was helpful and fun.
It was nice to try so many different things.
It was good to have hands-on experience.
It felt nice to be good at something.

Post 16

Oaklands Special School
Curriculum context: Work-related   *Activity:* Wheelchair User's Assistant Skills

This is a work-based learning programme where senior students (16–19) learn, practise, and have to pass a test in all the skills necessary to assist wheelchair users in school or at home. This helps pupils to:
- take responsibility for another person, relating to them in an empathetic way;
- practise the co-ordination skills necessary to push a wheelchair and its user and negotiate a variety of situations and environments with the need to keep a more dependent person safe;
- observe and then make allowances for the individual requirements of users and their chairs;
- fulfil a useful role successfully and learn skills which are applicable in many situations.

They also learn to overcome their own feelings of dependency, developing consideration for others; how to reassure others; to make quick decisions in the interests of safety; to co-operate with the wheelchair user and other assistants; to have a greater understanding of safety in mobility; to experience success, boosting self-esteem and confidence; to respect differences in requirements for mobility and health; and to have a positive attitude to work and to helping others.

Questions for reflection: Why does X have to use a wheelchair? How does he feel when being pushed?
What difficult situations might you meet?
Why must you talk to the user about what is happening?

Responses from pupils: He might feel nervous or scared; I didn't like it when I was being pushed.
If she has a fit I'll put on the brakes and fetch the nearest staff quickly.
I want to pass the test because I'm senior now/I can help others/It's like the staff/I want to be his friend.

Key stage 4

St Vincent de Paul RC High School
Curriculum context: Tutor period/whole school   ***Activity:*** School Council/Manchester Young People's Council

The School Council was set up in 1996 to enable students to take an active part in the school and have responsibility within its structures. All year groups were given the chance to hear the advantages and disadvantages of establishing a council and to discuss how to make it democratic and what it would do. After an overview, groups of students discussed and fed back ideas to their whole year group. Following a governors' meeting to discuss the school council, tutor groups designed posters to advertise it and met with school and advisory staff to plan an implementation schedule. A three-day election programme led to the students' vote. All students who stood for election received a certificate for their record of achievement. New council members were inducted and trained in peer-counselling skills, and regular staff and student support meetings and an ongoing evaluation process were established. The pupils also elected two representatives to the Manchester Young People's Council. This was set up by the City Council to give young people a voice on matters which affect their lives, to increase their awareness of democratic procedures and to encourage them to use their vote at 18. It meets termly. As part of the school's contribution, the pupils developed and led workshops for adults at three national and international conferences. Involvement in MYPC has empowered the pupils in many ways and given them a confidence that benefits their school work and self-esteem.

*These activities provide the **opportunities** for pupils to:*

a	take responsibility	√	f	develop relationships	√
b	feel positive about themselves	√	g	consider social and moral dilemmas	√
c	participate	√	h	ask for help/find information/provide advice	√
d	make real choices and decisions	√	i	prepare for change	√
e	meet and work with other people	√			

As a result of this activity the pupils have learnt the following:

Skills:
- to present themselves positively, confidently and appropriately with adults;
- to assess their own qualities;
- to join discussions through questioning, clarifying, listening and relevant responding;
- to co-operate with others in a team, completing the task and taking initiative;
- to manage time and organise poster and workshop activities;
- to use different approaches to decision-making, including democratic and consensus.

Knowledge:
- their personal strengths and weaknesses in new and challenging situations;
- how to respond when taking on responsibilities;
- the skills and qualities necessary for producing workshops for adults.

Attitudes and values:
- to appreciate and value the opinions and contributions of peers and adults;
- to respect peers and adults involved in the activities;
- the capacity to enjoy the experience.

Questions for reflection: How did you feel the planning sessions went?
What personal benefits have you gained from your experiences?
What was the greatest challenge for you? What did you enjoy most?
Would you do everything the same or change some things?

Responses from pupils: Could have possibly spent more time, but nothing prepares you for the real event.
Confidence in myself, speaking out for others and oneself.
Dealing with foreign visitors, ensuring they understood.
The presentation was not as daunting once it began.

This activity contributes to the following strands of the PSHE and Citizenship frameworks:

Personal development	√	Health and safety	√
Relationships	√	Active citizens	√

Appendix 3

Form A

School: Teacher:
Year/class: Curriculum context:

Activity (Opportunity for personal and social development)

---

*This activity provides the **opportunities** for pupils to:* (see page 19)

a	take responsibility	❏
b	feel positive about themselves	❏
c	participate	❏
d	make real choices and decisions	❏
e	meet and work with other people	❏

f	develop relationships	❏
g	consider social and moral dilemmas	❏
h	ask for help/find information/provide advice	❏
i	prepare for change	❏

As a result of this activity pupils will: (See key stage **learning outcomes** pages 24–31)

- be able to (skills):

- know and understand (knowledge):

- have thought about (attitudes and values):

Questions for reflection:

Responses from pupils:

This activity contributes to the following strands of the PSHE and Citizenship frameworks:

Personal development	❏	Health and safety	❏
Relationships	❏	Active citizens	❏

Form B

Step 1a: Identify pupils' needs and set priorities for personal and social development

PSHE and Citizenship Frameworks	Record priorities for the pupils' personal and social development
1 Develop confidence and responsibility and make the most of their abilities	*e.g. YR need to settle well into school*
2 Prepare to play an active role as citizens	*e.g. Y7 need to build on Y6 experience by giving pupils some real responsibility*
3 Develop a healthy, safer lifestyle	*e.g. Y6 need to complete preparation for puberty*
4 Develop good relationships and respect the differences between people	*e.g. Y10 need to counter homophobia, by helping pupils understand more about the diversity of sexual orientation and the effects of bullying*

Form C

Step 1b: Identify opportunities for personal and social development across the curriculum

PSHE Framework: Breadth of opportunities

During the key stage, pupils should be taught the knowledge, skills and understanding through opportunities to:

a take responsibility

b feel positive about themselves

c participate

d make real choices and decisions

e meet and work with other people

f develop relationships

g consider social and moral dilemmas

h ask for help/find information/provide advice

i prepare for change

In Year _____ the school provides the following opportunities for personal and social development:

Three contexts:	What opportunities are offered (a) – (i)?
1 **Designated time** (PSE/PSHE/circle time): *e.g. environment project*	*a, c, d, e, f, g, h*
2 **Subjects:** *e.g. literacy hour*	*b, h*
3 **Other activities:** *e.g. school council*	*a, c, d, e, f, g, h*

Identify enrichment opportunities during the year

Year group							
Residential							
Visits							
Visitors							
School council							
Theatre-in-education							
Work-related activities							
Health week							
Environment projects							
Community service							

Choose from these other activities and/or add your own:

Mini-enterprise	Industry day	Careers convention	Peer education	Junior citizenship	Positive rewards	Field trip
Work experience	Reception duty	Career interviews	Peer mentoring	Artist-in-residence	Special projects	

Form E

Plan the curriculum for PSD

Step 2: Priorities for personal and social development – identify what pupils should learn

1 Priorities for personal and social development Complete column 1 from Form B	2 Learning outcomes Identify learning outcomes using pages 24–31 and complete column 2	

Step 3: Determine the curriculum context and staff responsibility

3 Curriculum context	4 Responsibility
Complete column 3 using Forms C and D by selecting the best opportunity to meet the outcomes	Complete column 4 by recording the member of staff who will be responsible for this part of the curriculum

PASSPORT Project Advisory Committee

Chair:	Professor John Tomlinson CBE
Project leaders:	Jane Lees
	Sue Plant
Mick Baldwin	Palatine School, Worthing
Helen Brooks	Royton and Crompton School, Oldham
Jan Campbell	Hertfordshire Education Advisory Service
Helen Flynn	Observer, Teacher Training Agency
John Ford	Observer, Department for Education and Employment
Peter Griffiths	Observer, HMI, Office for Standards in Education
Miralee Hackshaw	Dalmain Primary School, Forest Hill, London
Jan Hamilton	Park Lane Primary School and Parents' Centre, Nuneaton
John Keast	Observer, Qualifications and Curriculum Authority
David Kerr	Citizenship and Education for Democracy Working Group
Simon Richey	Calouste Gulbenkian Foundation
Marianne Talbot	Spiritual, Moral, Social and Cultural Development in Schools Project, Qualifications and Curriculum Authority

PASSPORT Project Reference Group

The following organisations and individuals accepted the invitation to respond to the project at different stages of its development.

Teacher Associations

Association of Teachers and Lecturers
National Association of Education Inspectors, Advisers and Consultants
National Association of Head Teachers
National Association of Schoolmasters and Union of Women Teachers
Professional Association of Teachers
Secondary Heads Association

Other Professional Bodies

Antidote
Association of Religious Education Advisers, Inspectors and Consultants
British Educational Research Association
Catholic Education Service
Children's Rights Development Unit
Commission for Racial Equality
Council for Environmental Education
Department for Education and Employment Working Party on Citizenship
Drug Education Forum

Family Links
Jenny Mosley Associates
National Association of Governors and Managers
National Association of Pastoral Care in Education
National Children's Bureau
National Council for Voluntary Youth Services
National Educational Business Partnerships Network
National Health Education Liaison Group
National Standing Committee of Advisers, Inspectors and Consultants of PSE
National Youth Agency
Professional Council for Religious Education
Re:membering Education
Sex Education Forum
The Muslim College
The National Society

Individuals

Professor Ron Best, Faculty of Education, Roehampton Institute London
Alan Brown, Glasgow Caledonian University
Philip Hope MP
Daphne Learmont OBE
Professor Richard Pring, Department of Educational Studies, University of Oxford
Rachel Thomson, South Bank University
David Trainer
Dr Jasper Ungoed-Thomas
Chris Watkins, Institute of Education, London University
Professor Richard Whitfield

PASSPORT Project Development Schools

The following schools have been instrumental in guiding the project at each stage of its development:

Broadlands School, Bath and North East Somerset; Chewton Mendip CE VA Primary School, Somerset; Christ Church Primary School, Wandsworth; Cricket Green Special School, Mitcham; Grey Coat Hospital, Westminster; Hardenhuish School, Wiltshire; Ravenstone Primary School, Wandsworth

PASSPORT Project Pilot LEAs and Schools

Birmingham LEA	Bordesley Green Girls School; Fox Hollies Special School; Kingstanding Special School; Kingsthorne JI School; Stechford JI School; Wheelers Lane Boys School
Cambridgeshire LEA	Ernuf Community School; Eynesbury Primary School; Pepys Road Special School; Sir Harry Smith Community College; Spring Common Special School; Steeple Morden Primary School

Camden LEA	Argyle Primary School; Camden School for Girls; Chalcot School; Gospel Oak Primary School; Haverstock School; Swiss Cottage School
Devon LEA	Bidwell Brook Special School; Cullompton Community College; Ladysmith First School; Ratcliffe Special School; The Park School; Uffculme Primary School
Dudley LEA	Bromley Primary School; Cradley High School; Olive Hill Primary School; Ridgewood High School; Rosewood Special School; Sutton Special School
Gateshead LEA	Harlow Green Infant School; Hewarth Grange School; Hookergate School; Joseph Swan School; Lord Lawson of Beamish School; Ravensworth Terrace Primary School; Ryton Infant School; Ryton School; St Joseph's RC Primary School; Thomas Hepburn Community School; Whickham School
Hampshire LEA	Broughton Primary School; Hythe Primary School; Perins Community School; Porchester Community School; Whitedown Special School; Wolverdene Special School
Hertfordshire LEA	Batchwood Special School; Greenfields School; Lakeside School; Onslow St Audrey's School; St Mary's JM School; Westfield School
Hounslow LEA	Felton Community School; Heston Community School; Heston Junior School; Marjory Kinnon School; Oaklands Special School; Our Lady and St John RC JI/N School
Kingston LEA	Bedelsford School; Coombe Girls' School; St Matthew's School; St Paul's Primary School; St Phillip's School; Tolworth Girls' School
Kirklees LEA	Batley High School for Boys; Cawley Lane JI/N School; Crosland Moor Junior School; Highfields School; Howden Clough High School; Ravenham School; St Peter's CE (A) Primary School; Scissett Middle School
Lancashire LEA	Fishwicks County Primary School; Mount Carmel RC High School; Overton St Helens CE School; Sherburn School; Southlands High School
Lewisham LEA	Anerley Boys Secondary Residential EBD School; Baring School; Coopers Lane Primary School; Greenvale Secondary SLD School; Northbrooke CE (Mixed) School; The Centre Pupil Referral Unit; St Joseph's Academy
Manchester LEA	Bench Hill Junior School; Burnage High School; Holy Name RC Primary School; Roundwood Special School; St Vincent de Paul RC High School; Webster Primary School
Northamptonshire LEA	Barry Lower School; Billing Brook School; Campion School; Friars School; Latimer School
Rochdale LEA	Alderman Kay Special School; Brownhill Special School; Heywood Community School; Hopwood County Primary School; Lowerplace County Primary School; Matthew Moss High School
Shropshire and Telford and Wrekin LEAs	Corvedale CE (Aided) School; Red Hill Primary School; Severndale School; Southall School; Wakeman School; William Brookes School
Suffolk LEA	Birchwood County Primary School; Copleston High School; Great Cornard Upper School; Riverwalk Special School; The Ashley Special School; Westgate County Primary School
Tameside LEA	Dale Grove School; Egerton Park High School; Livingstone Primary School; Millbrook Primary School; Samuel Laycock School; Stamford High School
Wandsworth LEA	Alderbrook Primary School; Broadwater Primary School; Falconbrook Primary School; Fircroft Primary School; Furzedown Primary School; Heathmere Primary School; Hotham Primary School; Ravenstone Primary School; St Boniface Primary School; Sellincourt Primary School; Sir James Barrie Primary School; The Alton Primary School; The Vines Special School; Trinity St Mary's Primary School; Wandle Primary School
West Sussex LEA	Catherington School; Flora McDonald Junior School; Littlegreen School; London Meed Primary School; The Bourne Community College; Thomas Bennett Community College

We wish to thank the following people for responding to our request for advice and information and, in many instances, for sending us documentation to stimulate and inform our thinking:

Chris Addison, St Helens LEA; Chris Anderson, Sheffield LEA; David Andrews, NACGT; Hazel Ashley, Youth and Community Hertfordshire LEA; Sue Aucott, ROSPA; Roshan Bailey, Personal Finance Education Group; Lyn Banks, Northumberland LEA; Anthony Barnes, QCA; Phil Barnett, Health Education Unit Birmingham; Chris Beer, Swindon Health Promotion; Julia Bird, Sowelu Associates; Simon Blake, FPA; Nick Boddington, Essex LEA; Sandra Bourne, Enfield LEA; Sue Bowker, Health Promotion Wales; Dorit Braun, National Stepfamily Association; Miriam Brewis, Bedfordshire LEA; Sylvia Brown, Liverpool LEA; Terry Brown, Consultant; Ali Brownlie, Development Education Association; Kevin Buckle, Suffolk LEA; Mark Burns, Wearside NHS Trust; Denice Burton, Wiltshire Health Promotion; Liz Butterworth, Norfolk LEA; Fiona Carnie, Human Scale Education; Neil Casey, ACET; Colin Chapman, Redbridge Health Promotion; Peter Chell, South Staffordshire Health Authority; Sarah Clein, Trafford LEA; Elizabeth Collins, Bolton LEA; Janet Convery, Children and Violence Forum; Vanessa Cooper, Bromley LEA; Estelle Corbyn, Stokesley School, North Yorkshire; Geoffrey Court, Circle Works; Stephen Cox, OSIRIS Educational; Gillian Cunliffe, Brighton and Hove LEA; Maria D'Acampo, Raynes Park High School, Merton; Alun Davies, Gateshead LEA; Graham Davies, Cardiff LEA; Pru Davies, Vale of Glamorgan LEA; Hilary Dixon, Independent Consultant; Brian Dobson, Tacade; Melody Dougan, Consultant; Rob Eager, RSPCA; Janet Edwards, Centre for Citizenship Studies; Michelle Elliott, Kidscape; Antony Evans, South Gloucestershire LEA; Vivienne Evans, Tacade; K.B. Everard, Development Training Advisory Group; Sue Falconer, Hampshire LEA; Janet Farrell, Dukinfield LEA; Fiona Feehan, West Sussex LEA; Julia Fiehn, QCA; Pauline Forrest, Hampshire LEA; Gill Frances, Sex Education Forum; Ann Furedi, Birth Control Trust; Penny Gaunt, West Sussex LEA; Lynne Gerlach, Sowelu Associates; Dawn Gill, Doncaster LEA; Jan Goulstone, Hammersmith and Fulham LEA; Gráinne Graham, Salford and Trafford Health Promotion Service; John Hall, Childline;

Kevin Hart, Superintendent Manchester Police; Jenny Harmston, Swindon LEA/Health Promotion Service; Eileen Hayes, NSPCC; Carol Healy, Health Education Authority; Wendy Heron, Carmarthen LEA; Martin Hore, Outdoor Education Advisers Panel; M. Howell, Solihull LEA; John Huskins, Independent Consultant; Caroline Jamison, Hillingdon LEA; Margaret Jones, Northampton LEA; Sylvia Jones, Denbighshire LEA; Adrian King, Berkshire LEA; Diane King, Manchester IAS; Tony Leather, Young Enterprise; Mui Li, Harrow LEA; John Lloyd, Birmingham LEA; Eleonora Lockwood, East Surrey Health Promotion; Sylvia Lunn, Leeds LEA; Doreen Massey, Independent Consultant; Alison Matthews, QCA; Deborah Mbofana, Berkshire Health Authority; Pat McGill, Cheshire LEA; Lesley de Meza, Independent Consultant; Lyz Mitchell, Warwickshire LEA; Janet Moldauer, Royal College of Nursing; Alysoun Moon, Wessex Institute; Gill Morris, Camden LEA; Colin Noble, Kirklees LEA; Louise O'Connor, Roehampton Institute of Higher Education; Sue Orpin, Kent LEA; Louise Pankhurst, The Child Psychotherapy Trust; Martin Perry, Hope UK; Frances Phelps, Shropshire LEA; Kathy Portlock, Hounslow LEA; Chris Purves, North Essex LEA; Tony Pye, Health Promotion Calderdale; John Rees, APAUSE; Brenda Reid, Health First; Suzie Rheindorp, Relate; Michael Roberts, Life Education Centres; Don Rowe, Citizenship Foundation; June Sanderson, Bradford LEA; Kath Sanderson, Rochdale LEA; Lorna Scott, Independent Consultant; Dali Sidebottom, Avon Health Promotion; Maggie South, West Sussex Health Authority; Ina Standish, Blaenau Gwent LEA; Jacqui Stevens, Wiltshire LEA; Corinne Stevenson, Hounslow LEA; Steve Stillwell, Schools Industry Project; Annabel Talbot, Cambridge LEA; Marilyn Tew, Jenny Mosley Associates; Marilyn Toft, Lewisham LEA; Justin Tomkins, Grubb Institute; John Tripp, APAUSE; Kay Trotter, Kingston Education Business Partnership; Marion Waddington, Lancashire LEA; Chris Warner, Dudley LEA; Dilys Went, Trainer and Consultant; Murray White, International Council for Self-esteem; Roger White, ASDAN; Helena Williams, Devon LEA; Kath Wilson, Somerset LEA/Health Promotion; Paul Wotton, Metropolitan Police; Laurence Wrenne, Southwark LEA.

Appendix 3

References and sources

This list includes the materials used to help to develop the PASSPORT Framework for Personal and Social Development. We would like to thank everyone who generously supplied us with copies of their own schemes and materials, whether published or in draft form. Other texts provide a useful reference.

Aims of Citizenship Education, The, Don Rowe and Jan Newton. The Citizenship Foundation 1997

Animals and Education: Making your school animal-friendly. Royal Society for the Protection of Cruelty to Animals (no date)

Arrangements for Personal and Social Development: Higher Still Development Programme. Scottish Consultative Council on the Curriculum 1997

Citizenship at Key Stages 3 and 4: Initial guidance for schools. Qualifications and Curriculum Authority 2000

Citizenship Benchmarks (draft). Birmingham Education Department 1998

Curriculum for Global Citizenship, A (extract). Oxfam Development Education Programme 1997

Curriculum Guidance 4: Education for Economic and Industrial Understanding
Curriculum Guidance 5: Health Education
Curriculum Guidance 7: Environmental Education
Curriculum Guidance 8: Education for Citizenship. National Curriculum Council 1990

Curriculum Planning: Subject Guidance PSHE. London Borough of Southwark

Curriculum 3–5 based on 'Desirable Outcomes'. Warwickshire County Council

Developing Effective Classroom Groups, Gene Stanford, adapted by Pam Stoate. Acora Books 1991

Education for Citizenship and the Teaching of Democracy in Schools: Consultation paper. Qualifications and Curriculum Authority 1998

Education for Sustainable Development in the Schools Sector: A Report to DfEE/QCA from the Panel for Education for Sustainable Development. Council for Environmental Education, the Development Education Association, RSPB and WWF-UK 1998

Equal Opportunities Guidelines. West Sussex County Council 1998

Framework for the Assessment of Personal and Social Development. Hertfordshire County Council Education 1998

Good Practice in Drug Education and Prevention series:
The Right Choice: Guidance on selecting drug education materials
The Right Approach: Quality standards in drug education
The Right Responses: Managing and making policy for drug-related incidents in schools. Standing Conference on Drug Abuse 1998–9

Guidance for schools on managing the development of a framework for improving employability through the curriculum at key stage 4 (draft text). Qualifications and Curriculum Authority 1997

Health Education: A Framework for Primary Schools. Redbridge and Waltham Forest Health Authority 1998 (revised edition)

Health for Life 1: A teacher's planning guide to health education in the primary school, Health Education Authority. Thomas Nelson and Sons Ltd 1989

Heart of the Matter, The. Scottish Consultative Council on the Curriculum 1995

Industry and the curriculum 5–14: Guidance for teachers, D. Smith, A. Ross and A. Miller. Centre for Education and Industry, University of Warwick 1993

Learning by Heart: The Role of Emotional Education in Raising School Achievement. Co-ordinated by Re:membering Education, initiated and funded by the Calouste Gulbenkian Foundation 1998

Learning Framework for Personal Finance, A. Personal Finance Education Group 1998

Learning Outcomes from Careers Education and Guidance. Qualifications and Curriculum Authority 1999

National Curriculum, The: Handbook for primary teachers in England – Key Stages 1 and 2
National Curriculum, The: Handbook for secondary teachers in England – Key Stages 3 and 4. Department for Education and Employment and Qualifications and Curriculum Authority 1999

National Healthy School Standard: Getting Started – A guide for schools
National Healthy School Standard: Guidance. Department for Education and Employment 1999

On the Side of Young People: Your Guide to the Schools Involvement Programme. Metropolitan Police 1997

Opening Doors: A framework for developing career-related learning in primary and middle schools, Bill Law and Barbara McGowan. CRAC/The National Institute for Careers Education and Counselling 1999

Pathways Toward Adult Life: A Curriculum Framework and Management Guide for Schools, London Enterprise Agency. Kogan Page 1997

PEPP: Personal Effectiveness in Primary Pupils – A Guide for Teachers. Kingston Education Business Partnership

Personal and Social Development: 5–14 National Guidelines.
  The Scottish Education Department 1993

Personal and Social Development 5–14 Exemplification: The Whole School Approach – A Staff Development Workshop.
  Scottish Consultative Council on the Curriculum (no date)

Personal and Social Education: Primary Framework
Personal and Social Education: Secondary Framework.
  St Helens Metropolitan Borough Council 1998

Personal and Social Education across the Curriculum: Curriculum and Assessment Guidelines.
  London Borough of Merton 1994

Personal and Social Education and Equal Opportunities: Scheme of work for primary schools (extract).
  Shropshire County Council 1996

Personal and Social Education Curriculum Framework: Key Stages 1 to 4.
  Brighton & Hove/East Sussex County Council

Personal and Social Education from 5–16: Curriculum Matters 14 (An HMI series).
  Department of Education and Science, HMSO 1989

Personal, Social and Health Education and Citizenship at Key Stages 1 and 2: Initial guidance for schools.
  Qualifications and Curriculum Authority 2000

Personal, Social and Health Education at Key Stages 3 and 4: Initial guidance for schools.
  Qualifications and Curriculum Authority 2000

Planning for Learning: Piecing Together the National Curriculum Jigsaw – Health Education.
  London Borough of Lewisham

Preparation for Working Life: Guidance for schools on managing a co-ordinated approach to work-related learning at key stage 4.
  Qualifications and Curriculum Authority 1999

Preparing Young People for Adult Life: A report of the National Advisory Group on Personal, Social and Health Education.
  Department for Education and Employment 1999

Progression Guidance for PSHE (extract).
  Cambridge County Council

Promotion of Pupils' Spiritual, Moral, Social and Cultural Development, The (draft guidance).
  Qualifications and Curriculum Authority 1998

PSE Outcomes. Kirklees Education Authority

PSHE Curriculum Map. London Borough of Hillingdon

Quality Work with Young People: Developing social skills and diversion from risk. John Huskins 1998

Skills for Choice: Developing pupils' career management skills.
  School Curriculum and Assessment Authority 1996
  (available from Qualifications and Curriculum Authority)

Skills for Life: A whole school approach to personal and social development at key stages 3 and 4. Tacade 1994

Skills for the Primary School Child: Promoting the protection of children. Tacade 1990

Teaching Environmental Matters through the National Curriculum.
  School Curriculum and Assessment Authority 1996

Teaching for Effective Learning.
  Scottish Consultative Council on the Curriculum 1996

Teenage Pregnancy. Social Exclusion Unit 1999

'Values and educating the whole person', Professor B.J. McGettrick, from *Perspectives: A series of occasional papers on values and education.*
  Scottish Consultative Council on the Curriculum 1995

The table showing Pupils' Needs and Priorities at Key Stages 1–4 (page 18) is based on research data from the following sources:
Exploring Health Education: A growth and development perspective, Health Education Authority. Macmillan 1990

Key Data on Adolescence, John Coleman.
  Trust for the Study of Adolescence 1997

Young People and Health: The health behaviour of school-aged children. Health Education Authority 1997

Young People and Illegal Drugs into 2000, John Balding.
  Schools Health Education Unit, Exeter 2000

Young People, Drugs and Drugs Education: Missed opportunities – Executive briefing, Louise O'Connor.
  Roehampton Institute London 1997

Young People in 1996, John Balding.
  Schools Health Education Unit, Exeter 1997

Young People in 1997, John Balding.
  Schools Health Education Unit, Exeter 1998

Young People in 1998, John Balding.
  Schools Health Education Unit, Exeter 1999

Youth Values: Identity, diversity and social change,
  J. Holland and R. Thomson. Economic and Social Research Council funded project #129251020